HOW
TO REACH THE
FOURTH DIMENSION

Rx:
TRY CONCEPT-THERAPY

By

Dr. H. M. A. van Ginkel

DeVorss & Co., *Publishers*
4900 Eagle Rock Blvd.
Los Angeles, Calif. 90041

Printed in the United States of America
DeVorss & Co., 4900 Eagle Rock Blvd., Los Angeles, Calif. 90041

TABLE OF CONTENTS

*"Condemnation Without
Investigation is the
Mark of Ignorance."*

FOREWORD

An ancient sage once counseled his followers: "A journey of a thousand miles begins with a single step." True it is, but how difficult it may sometimes be to take that first step, especially if it is in the direction of making changes in our personality or in the manner of living which has become habitual with us.

About a year ago a friend of mine stopped by my home for a few moments' visit. During the course of conversation she told me about a young optometrist she had recently met and described him as a very personable, dynamic young man, with a good mind, but a man beset with difficulties and problems of a spiritual and emotional nature. A short time later in a strange coincidence I did indeed meet this young man, and the above description proved to be quite accurate. As he poured out his heart to me in a subsequent conversation, I marvelled at how one plagued with so many real, harsh problems could still maintain any degree of emotional balance. He and his problems were born together in Europe at the height of the World War II conflict. Tossed from pillar-to-post, attic-to-stable, unwanted and unappreciated as a living human soul, his was an existence of complete insecurity and rejection by all he beheld. Body and soul were held together only by an indomitable will to live. To keep the tiny spark of life aflame was his only desire. I will not pursue this thought further. He would not want it so. I mention these things only to give you a picture of his troubled beginnings.

The young man's name was Dr. H. M. A. van Ginkel. I call him Hank. His full name, like his early history, seems much too long and difficult. He began to study the courses of instruction sponsored by the Concept-Therapy Institute. I have watched him struggle in his understanding, fighting his way slowly over obstacle after obstacle. His one burning desire became—and is now—to reshape, re-mould and refine his whole personality, both the inner and the outer man. His goal is no longer the fight to change the world to his point of view, but the battle to conquer himself, so that he can adapt himself to our world as it is and feel at home in, and at one with this universe as the Creator made it.

This book is uniquely his own work, a part of the story of his progression through life as his own eyes now see it. It is, of course, purely a personal viewpoint, but it is one story which I think you will enjoy reading. He is well on his way out of his confining shell, and this book shows but one of his many unique talents. He knew very little about the structure of any literary work, but here is his book, like one facet of a diamond, just to let us all know that it can be done. He has also become an accomplished lecturer on many interesting subjects from a wide variety of fields of science and philosophy, and especially his favorite "Philosophy of Life"—Concept Therapy.

I may not whole-heartedly agree with all his personal viewpoints contained in the book, but neither will I violently disagree. Each man's thought is his very own property, and none of us can ever completely understand another. What seems important to me is that his goals, his reasoning and his actions are now of a high, constructive, and lawful order. I have personally beheld the steps of progress described herein. They are real.

I have a strong premonition that one day soon, our friend Hank may be back at his desk again, hard at work on another book, so that the world may learn more about his progress through his beloved Concept-Therapy studies. I hope that in these pages you will come to know and respect him as I do.

Charles Craig

WHAT'S CONCEPT-THERAPY
ALL ABOUT?

Though it presumes to take no sides, this book may be called a "boatrocker." Its ideas, concepts, and contentions are based upon Truth, and Truth has always rocked the boat, for It is against all "sides," by the mere fact that It recognizes no such thing as "sides." Sooner or later, and hopefully sooner, we will all line up and squarely gaze upon its face; and when we do, our road to Freedom will have become reality. Throughout the centuries, we have tacitly allowed ourselves to be led astray by our two major sources of knowledge, namely Science and Religion. Individual intelligence, however, has now reached the point were many sound-thinking people are beginning to seriously question the validity of such authority in respect to human emotions, conduct, and life. If you are among those people, this book is for you. To quote Dr. Fleet, founder of CONCEPT-THERAPY, on the subject: "With the progress of civilization, and the general growth and diffusion of intelligence everywhere, there is one problem upon which all else focalizes, though the fact seems to be seldom apprehended or clearly realized. Not only do science and religion face each other at one point, but the life of each is—at that one point—involved. It is not only the often recognized conflict between religion and science — which was long ago worn threadbare — it is the fact that both science and religion are out of joint with themselves: the battle ground may — in a broad sense—be named psychology.

All problems and all discussions of the *real issues* arise

from, involve, or center around the nature, laws that govern, and destiny of the human soul.

From the very nature of these problems, their intricacy and diversity, they remain the latest in the categories of science to be seriously investigated. For the same reason, they have been the subject of dogma and revelation in religion, with doors slammed in the face of all investigation, as not only useless, but wicked, and often dangerous.

Between the agnosticism of science, and the dogmatism of religion, knowledge has been crucified, and there it hangs today, a curse to the one, and a cross to the other; the same problem, only facing different ways. And yet, the reconciliation is not far to seek.

Science and religion represent different departments in human interest, and in the life of man. So far as they are each true, they must eventually and inevitably clasp hands, instead of working at cross purposes. Actual knowledge of the human soul, as a science of psychology on the one hand and the duty of man to himself, to his fellows and to his God and the destiny of the human soul as essential religion on the other hand, must constitute the basis of union and the point of agreement."

"There is every evidence that men of science and men of religion, in the study of psychiatry and metaphysics, are getting closer and closer to a real understanding of this great problem."

"The accredited psychology of today, however, has hitherto failed to demonstrate any actual knowledge of the human soul, or even to postulate its existence as a fact in nature. The theologies and religions of today appeal largely to superstition and fear and support their dogmas by revelations—the diverse interpretations of which have segregated religion into a large number of sects with no bond or union or basis of agreement between them.

As yet, neither science nor theology pretends to give us any real information of the human soul. Science says frankly that she does not know. Theology bids us believe and obey, trust and hope. Philosophy speculates and reasons. Science must deal with facts, demonstrate their actuality and classify them—that is—find their natural order and sequence. In psychology, the facts are within the realms of consciousness and therefore their demonstration is a matter of individual experience. That is why psychology differs from all other sciences. *No one* can transfer his individual experience to another — he can describe how he gained it and give the result and conclusion, but for the student or patient to learn anything, he himself must have the experience. We don't *really know* anything except that which we have gained through *personal experience. Real knowledge* comes, and can come, in no other way. No teacher of real science or psychology can ever transmit or transfer his knowledge to another. All he can do is to describe the method and the steps by which he acquired it, and assist the student in acquiring it for himself in the same way or under the same processes and LAWS. We have only to reflect on the ordinary experiences of life to realize that this is a *universal principle* and rule. In the deeper science of the soul and in the higher life, instead of this law being relaxed it becomes all the more binding. Do not the principles that adhere the atoms and the molecules still hold in the world and solar systems? Is not this precisely what is meant by the Reign of Law? If man were built upon some other scheme or plan than the rest of nature, how could he apprehend or adjust himself to nature? The very concept of miracle is lawlessness. Mystery is just another name for ignorance. *Knowledge,* however, means the *experience* and apprehension of Law. Neither can the Laws of Nature and the Laws of God be at cross purposes for that would make harmony impossible and inconceivable. The confusion and discord are in all of us, and our work of CONCEPT-THERAPY and CONCEPTOLOGY means adjustment, harmony and then True Knowledge. It is the journey of the human soul on the royal highway to light, liberation, and eternal day."

The dictionary defines "CONCEPT" as: "an abstract general notion or conception, e.g. idea," and "THERAPY" as "having healing qualities, a working with," etc. In this light, CONCEPT-THERAPY may be defined as "working with concepts in the mind, or with ideas," in the sense of healing erroneous concepts and ideas. It teaches us how we all have concepts operating in our subconscious mind which influence our life, happiness, well-being, etc. We may be totally unaware (consciously) of the existence of such concepts, but that does not stop them from operating. If, for instance, the basic concept is that you can't be happy for more than two hours at a time, then the subsconscious mind will see to it that such a condition is manifested in your life, no matter how anxiously (consciously) you may wish to change that condition. If, however, you could find a way to change the BASIC CONCEPT, (and CONCEPT-THERAPY has found that way) you'd be on the road to permanent happiness. CONCEPT-THERAPY explains what constitutes the mind — how it tricks us, and how we can control it, thus changing our attitude — no longer allowing things to "get us down."

It delves into depth as to how the personality functions, and it dispels all of the mystery of hypnosis, replacing mystery with precious knowledge. It shows you how to change your thinking from negative to positive, and thus changes your entire life for the better. For instance, we all have become the victims of "compartmentalized thinking" at one time or another, and lack self-confidence in direct proportion to the degree that we are victims. For example, most people will say:

> "I am afraid I won't get that job," before even *trying*, or, "I am afraid of what he might say," or, "I am afraid I won't pass that test," or, upon failing one test, will say, "I am a failure," instead of saying, "I failed that one test, but that does not mean I am a failure: I'll just study harder next time," etc.

All of these are examples of how we've learned to use our imaging faculty negatively. CONCEPT-THERAPY teaches you how to say with faith and confidence:

> "I will get that job," and you will *get* it, or "I'll listen to what he has to say: if it's valid, I'll reconsider, if not, I'll do it my way," or "I *will* pass that test," and you will.

One of the most important tools is the effective use of your imagination, (not daydreaming, but *image-ing*), for it makes no difference to the subconscious whether an experience is real or imagined. In reference to synthetic experiencing, Maxwell Maltz in *Psycho-Cybernetics* mentions that we can become successful by experiencing the *feeling* of success. He states that: "Memories of past successes act as built-in stored information which gives us self-confidence for the present task." CONCEPT-THERAPY gives us that *feeling,* over and over again, until we rightfully feel that nothing can stop us. It simply becomes a matter of counter-balancing and overcoming the memories of past failures and mistakes by future memories of success and right action, laid down in the present. Just as we can block out the enormity of the sun by holding up a small, thin dime in front of our eye, so do we block out our enormous potential by permitting thoughts of failure — perpetuated and kept alive by subconscious "failure concepts"— to sway us and take hold of us. Parabolically speaking, CONCEPT-THERAPY shows us how to make the dime recede further and further away from us until it is no longer visible, having become absorbed by the vast Oneness of the Sun. As it recedes, our *inward perception* of the Sun becomes clearer and clearer, until at last it overtakes us, and we become the Sun Itself.

It asks you to accept nothing on blind faith, but it emphasizes the need for a thorough understanding of what is happening and why. There was, for instance, the case of the woman who had a severe backache, which responded to no treatment any doctor could give her. Fortunately, she was finally placed under the care of a doctor who knew about the influence of mental concepts upon the physical body. It turned out that her brother with his wife and two children had moved into the house, and — since he was out of work — depended upon her for support. The woman consciously kept thinking to herself: "I am carrying a great load," which thought became lodged in the subconscious mind and was finally expressed in the body as a pain in the back, as if she'd been carrying an actual physical load! Many phenomena which defy all pre-conceived notions — and which therefore require an open mind to properly interpret them — are taking place daily. An example of this is the case of the hypnotist who, after having hypnotized his subject, touched a pencil to his hand and told him that it was a burning cigarette.

Having the notion or idea in his mind that the "cigarette" would cause a blister to appear, the subject promptly raised a blister! Carrying the experiment a step further, the hypnotist then touched a burning cigarette to the other hand, but told the subject that it was a pencil. This time no blister appeared; in fact, no trace of a burn could be found anywhere! This experiment points out the truism that we are all hypnotized to a certain extent, and that the process of hypnosis is really one of *dehypnosis*, in so far that it awakens us to our own tremendous potential. We have all hypnotized ourselves into believing that we can do far less than that which we are actually capable of and all we need to do to realize our own potential is to rid our-selves of limiting concepts.

To the extent that we are able to dehypnotize ourselves, new horizons will open up to us, and sorrow and suffering will give way to happiness and freedom. I dedicate this book to that end, and gratefully acknowledge the help I have received in my own dehypnotization process from the CONCEPT-THERAPY INSTITUTE, Route 8, Box 250, San Antonio, Texas 78228. Should you wish to learn more about the institute, and the new way of life it can offer you, I encourage you to drop a post card to the above address, requesting a package of free literature and in-formation about informative lectures in your area. I can say that you'll be very happy you did!

Chapter One

"PEACE"

REFLECTION

As the Sun is reflected in the ocean droplets, so is the Divine reflected in each Soul. Just as the Sun and Moon can but partially reflect in cloudy waters, Divine Spirit can find but limited expression through cloudy minds.

As the dew covers but cannot conceal the reflection of the new day's dawn upon the tender young leaf, the dawn of Cosmic Day is reflected within man's Soul. It is thus that the eyes reflect the Soul, which in turn reflects the Spirit.

If you want a teacher, let Nature teach you to recognize the Divine in the undraped windows of the eyes of your fellow man.

I am a seeker. I suppose I always have been. In my childhood my mother frequently remarked that I had more questions than she or anyone could ever answer— and looking at it in restrospect I must admit that she was right. I must have questioned everything under the sun.

I was an avid swimmer as a young child, and on my frequent trips to one of Holland's many canals I used to hold my breath, get underneath the surface and attempt to figure out just where the very top of the water started! For, I reasoned, I can only look at the bottom of it, and looking at it this way I could never see the very top, because that which I was looking at always represented the bottom part of the top surface. I'd take my finger and carefully touch the water surface from above, but that would ruin the experiment, for the minute my finger touched the water, it would no longer be at the very top of the surface, but rather on the "bottom side" of it. Luckily, after some six months of attempting to find the answer to this self-created problem—and being unable to discuss it with anyone else—my many interests were gradually absorbed in other directions, and I abandoned my quest for an answer. Little did I know I'd never abandon the Quest Itself however. The problems simply became more complex and more seemingly unsolvable as I grew up. My perception of the world about me was such that, while on one hand I was extremely sensitive about my surroundings—much more so than my 'buddies,' etc., —on the other hand I was what may be referred to as very dense; refusing to acknowledge that which I did not wish to see. As a result I was in inner conflict and turmoil most of the time.

Not knowing what to do vocationwise, I altered my

ambition from welder to draughtsman to engineer and so on, and held a great variety of jobs ranging from machine-shop work to being a "wiper" in the merchant marines on the Holland-America Line.

At nineteen I decided I'd seen enough of the world and emigrated to America, hoping there to find greater freedom as well as the answers to my many questions. Since I still hadn't decided upon a career, I thought it would be best to volunteer for the draft, and decide upon a future career while I was getting my Army obligation out of the way. Within four months Uncle Sam responded; I underwent basic training in Fort Ord, Calif., then was sent to Fort Lewis, Wash., where we did nothing but take daily trips to the motor pool to sandpaper and grease various parts of the trucks. Complaining about it, I was sent to medical corpsman training school by my unit, only to be informed upon my return that I had been transferred to a "gung-ho" infantry outfit — in which neither my driver-training nor medical corpsman training would be of any use. There were many such discrepancies, and these occurrences didn't stop my questions about "the meaning of it all." I kept hearing about the "bad" enemy (the nationality of whom changes from time to time, some former enemies becoming friends and vice versa) and the good, pure and guileless American soldier system, which "never attacks first, but always defends itself in the face of extreme and intolerable provocation."

During bayonet practice, I was expected to demonstrate perfect and ruthless killer instinct, at the risk of being derided for non-compliance. More than once I observed officers becoming livid with rage if some lower rank soldier forgot to salute them, causing me to wonder about the leadership qualifications of men that were so vain and so easily disturbed. "Upholster a fence as plushly as you please, but when one group of men under some pretense or another sets itself apart from another group of men, expecting the other group to "look up" to them in some form or another, it is hard to say who is being locked in, and who is being locked out," I used to paraphrase Guy Endore. While in the Army I decided to take classes such as English, Algebra, Geometry, etc., in order to obtain an American high school diploma equivalent. Having abandoned the possibilities of welding, accounting, engineering, etc., and having become thoroughly disillusioned with all forms of medicine as I observed it being practiced in the Fort Lewis hospital, I decided upon a career as a non-medical doctor, and chose the field of optometry.

Being discharged in the early spring of 1960, I planned to start college in the fall of that year. One of the several jobs I held in the interim was the selling of encyclopedias; which endeavor lasted about two weeks, because I couldn't "stomach" the outright lies we were expected to tell people in our "sales pitch" (though the company had it cleverly figured out so as to be virtually unreproachable from a legal point of view by leaving themselves several "outs"). To me such tactics represented moral degradation of the subtlest yet vilest sort. During this time I met and married my now ex-wife, and adopted her four children. Our marriage was distinctly unhappy. The pressure of going through school, living in paper-thin walled university housing, and being plagued with an almost constant lack of sufficient money did not help matters. Upon the completion of my schooling, I hung out my doctor's shingle and enjoyed almost instantaneous success. Not being content with the

routine practice of optometry, and realizing that the eyes
are the only organs in the body where the conscious and
subconscious mechanisms work in unison—I decided to
study further into the relation between visual-perceptual
performance as it relates to reading performance. Finding such correlation to be very high, I then added a vision
and perception training section to my office, simultaneous-
ly adding yet another equipment loan to my already tower-
ing financial obligations. Instead of getting better, as we
had hoped, things steadily worsened at home, and finally
we decided to obtain a divorce.

It was along that time of my life that all of my
accumulated personal frustrations and pent-up emotions
"came to a head." I simply had to find answers to this
seemingly meaningless existence, and I was prepared to
go to any lengths to get to the bottom of such questions as:
"Who am I, why am I here, where am I going, what is
the meaning of it all—just what is the sense of life—
and living; of working at your career only to come home
to an empty emotional life—what's the use of getting
married, if you're going to get divorced or wind up fighting, anyway, etc., etc.," I later discovered that all the time
the trouble had lain with my Basic CONCEPTS of Life,
and that I was getting out of life exactly what I unconsciously expected.

In any case I began my quest in earnest now. Going
from one organization to another, visiting therapy groups,
"headshrinkers," etc., etc., I soon came to the realization
that there simply weren't any organizations that could
provide me with all of the answers. I therefore contented
myself with the idea that henceforth I would simply try
to get as much out of any one philosophy as possible and

attempt to fill in all the pieces as I went along. Then one day a patient of mine recommended CONCEPT-THER-APY. From her description, it sounded as though it made sense to me, but in the final analysis I figured it'd be just another one of those regular therapy groups, and being busily absorbed in my post-divorce emotional problems (which I refused to recognize at the time) I decided that I'd probably take it some time in the future. Adjusting to once again being alone—after seven years of marriage with an instant family—and attempting to solve many other problems that kept bombarding me, my life became increasingly complex, and I became more and more tense and irritable. Dr. Graig, the local instructor, invited me to attend a CONCEPT-THERAPY class to be given in December, and I would have gone if it were not for the fact that I had already decided to "escape" my problems temporarily by visiting my family in Holland over the Christmas holidays. (It was on this trip that my brother and I "conceived" of the interpretation of the Creation story in the second chapter). Though the trip succeeded in "getting my mind off things" for a while, I found upon returning that my problems were still very much here, and as ever were in urgent need of solving. By this time I had begun to anticipate the teaching of the next CONCEPT-THERAPY class, but found to my dismay that due to the scheduling of other classes, the instructers wouldn't be able to teach the class for another three months.

After three months of eternity, the date finally arrived. Yvonne Graig, one of the instructors, said, "people can get as little or as much out of our classes as they are prepared to receive. Some come with only a thimble to be filled, while others come with a 50 gallon barrel." I came with a 100 gallon drum.

I cannot tell you precisely what happened in that class, other than to say that the longing, seeking, striving, and yearning of my life was beginning to be satisfied. I was continuously bombarded by realizations which in essence all told me: "This is It," and: "This answers all of the questions I've raised all of these years," and so on. I learned that my present position was one I had created within my own thinking, and that throughout life we draw to us what we expect and no more, according to the BASIC CONCEPTS that we hold in our subconscious mind. Consciously, we may be completely unaware of the presence of such basic, limiting concepts, however, since we have long ago forgotten their basic cause and have subsequently repressed them from memory. The limiting process usually commences when a young child, who up to that time has felt unlimited in power, expression, and imagination, comes into contact with the "do's" and "don'ts", and "cans" and "can'ts," his future confidence in his ability to do anything often being in direct proportion to the frequency with which such limitations were sprinkled upon him in childhood, thus robbing him of the priceless self-confidence that comes through uninhibited expression. This made good sense to me, for I had become aware of a certain pattern in my life: While I had always been successful on a business and professional level, I had been equally unsuccessful when it came to long-lasting personal relationships. Apparently this was the BASIC CONCEPT which was operating in my life. Imagine my happy surprise when I was told that we could change these BASIC CONCEPTS, and not only was the class informed of that tremendous fact, but we were told HOW to do it!

I was taught the seven Universal Laws as originally proposed by the immortal genius of Hermes, beautifully adapted by CONCEPT-THERAPY in such a way as to enable all of us to learn to apply these Laws in our individual lives in order to change them for the better. Furthermore I was given a book in which were listed the laws of the body, mind, and soul, which—to the extent that they are obeyed—lead one directly into health, happiness, and peace of mind.

At the end of that first class I hardly knew myself. Having always been a very skeptical individual, the proposals and precepts discussed in the class were so rigorously logical yet at the same time so awe-inspiringly beautiful as well as simply overwhelming in implied importance that I just sat there in open-mouthed amazement, being overcome with pure joy. Something else had begun to vibrate within me, and that was a feeling of FAITH. To me, this was IT, and all I had to do now was to gain the KNOWLEDGE that CONCEPT-THERAPY recommended. Right on the spot I decided to enroll in the next class—Phase 1, in order to learn how to contact and direct the POWER WITHIN. (This turned out to be one of the most awe-inspiring classes I've ever attended in my life). However, because of the scheduling of other classes, Phase I wouldn't be taught locally for some time to come, and I decided that rather than waiting for it, I'd travel to Headquarters to take it. Being almost unconcerned as to what might happen to my office, I scheduled out two entire months with the express purpose in mind of spending that time at CONCEPT-THERAPY Headquarters in an effort to advance my knowledge. I went there with the objective of "soaking in the atmosphere," and to take as many classes as I could, for I simply had to have the knowledge, come what may.

How does one verbalize the gradual yet perceptible translation of a 30 year old boy into a 30 year old man?

Gradually I began to realize that all of Life's trouble is really opportunity in workclothes. I was reminded of a Chinese proverb; "If you plan for a year, plant grain; if you plan for ten years, plant a tree; if you plan for a hundred years, plant men."

The sage says: "Why not plan for all three, and grow grain and trees and men—for a complete life?"

Angela Morgan summed it up about as beautifully as I have ever seen it, in her poem:

WHEN NATURE WANTS A MAN

When Nature wants to drill a man
And thrill a man,
And skill a man.
When Nature wants to mold a man to play
the noblest part;
When she yearns with all her heart
To create so great and bold a man
That all the world shall praise—
Watch her method, watch her ways!
How she ruthlessly perfects
Whom she royally elects;
How she hammers him and hurts him,
And with mighty blows converts him
Into trial shapes of clay which only
Nature understands—

While his tortured heart is crying
and he lifts beseeching hands!—
How she bends, but never breaks,
When his good she undertakes . . .
How she uses whom she chooses
And with every purpose fuses him.
By every art induces him
To try his splendor out—
Nature knows what she's about.
When Nature wants to take a man,
And shake a man,
And wake a man;
When Nature wants to make a man,
To do the Future's will;
When she tries with all her skill
And she yearns with all her soul
To create him large and whole . . .

With what cunning she prepares him!
How she goads and never spares him,
How she whets him, and she frets him,
And in poverty begets him . . .
How she often disappoints whom she
sacredly anoints
With what wisdom she will hide him,
Never minding what betide him
Though his genius sob with slighting and his pride
may not forget!
Bids him struggle harder yet.
Makes him lonely
So that only
God's high messages shall reach him.
So that she may surely teach him,
What the Hierarchy planned.
Though he may not understand,
Gives him passions to command.
How remorselessly she spurs him

With terrific ardor stirs him
When she poignantly prefers him!

When Nature wants to name a man
And fame a man
And tame a man;
When Nature wants to shame a man
To do his heavenly best . . .
When she tries the highest test
That she reckoning may bring—
When she wants a god or king!
How she reins him and restrains him
So his body scarce contains him
While she fires him
And inspires him!

Keeps him yearning, ever burning for a tantalizing
goal—
Lures and lacerates his soul.
Sets a challenge for his spirit.
Draws it higher when he's near it—
Makes a jungle, that he clear it;
Makes a desert that he fear it
And subdue it if he can—
So doth Nature make a man.
Then to test his spirit's wrath
Hurls a mountain in his path—
Puts a bitter choice before him
And relentlessly stands o'er him.
"Climb, or perish!" so she says . . .
Watch her purpose, watch her ways!

Nature's plan is wondrous kind
Could we understand her mind . . .
Fools are they who call her blind.
When his feet are torn and bleeding
Yet his spirit mounts unheeding,

All his higher powers speeding,
Blazing newer paths and fine;
When the force that is divine
Leaps to challenge every failure and his ardor still
is sweet
And love and hope are burning in the presence of
defeat...
Lo, the crisis, lo the shout
That must call the leader out.
When people need salvation
Doth he come to lead the nation...
Then doth Nature show her plan
When the world has found—A MAN.

Angela Morgan

It is strange, I thought to myself, but by the time a
man can finally stand up and say: "I am a Man," he
no longer feels the need to do so.

Within two days upon my arrival at the *Ranch*, as
World Headquarters is called, things began to change.
For one thing I lost my usual anxiety, and began to feel
a PEACE which can not be expressed in words. As I
stayed, I learned more and more about the Universal
Laws, and learned from Dr. Schenk, the Institute's presi-
dent, how the Law of Electricity by comparison works
just as well for an eight year old boy as it does for any
electronic genius. For, even though he knows nothing of
the laws by which electricity operates, a ten ton elevator
will move just as quickly when the boy pushes the button
as it does for any adult. By the same token, however, the
Law, being impersonal, will strike the boy dead if he

should stick his fingers into the socket. For the LAW operates, whether we are ignorant of it or not. I thus began to understand that the LAW is our judge, and PAIN is the judgment. "The more I learn about these laws," I said to myself, "the more I can make them work for me by putting them to constructive use in my life! Gradually I began to learn how to work with the laws, one of them being the law of vibration. I was told how all living creatures are sensitive to vibration, animals as well as humans. (Most of us have had experience with this law when we walked into a house and almost immediately "sensed" the mood there, even though no one present said anything in particular, etc.)

"If you vibrate LOVE," said Opal Striffler, one of the Institute's excellent and very dedicated teachers, "people and animals around you will 'pick up' on it, and be drawn towards you, but if you vibrate HATE or ANGER, you don't need to say a word, for very quickly they'll perceive that too and stay away from you."

At this point I remembered having read about "mental health" clinics for pets, in which the attending doctors had begun to insist that rather than the pet itself, its owner should be treated for whatever neurosis was ailing the pet, since it can only have "picked up" such psychological problems from its owner(s)! Having had experiences with people before, I did not question the workings of the Law one bit, but I was a bit skeptical about its application to animals. I decided to experiment. The next morning I woke up at 4:30, and it seemed as though I was drawn out of bed by some irresistible force, which inclined me to get dressed and take a walk. Being in a somewhat drowsy and confused state of mind, I stepped out into the as yet semi-dark morning, blinking a few times in an effort to get my eyes adjusted to the twilight.

After having walked a while, I was suddenly aware of the presence of an animal. Having never seen one before, I searched my memory banks for the pictorial representation I had once seen of the armadillo. Try as I might, I couldn't remember whether they were supposed to be dangerous or not, and so I was confused not knowing whether to act friendly, stop walking, or to head the other way. The armadillo turned and looked at me, or rather pointed its peculiarly shaped nose in my direction, and as if on cue we both stopped dead in our tracks. We must have stood there transfixed, silently looking at each other, for a very long 20 seconds or so, after which it took several steps away from me, alternately looking towards and away from my direction. Likewise I took a few steps toward it—feeling strangely excited by it all—after which we again stopped and looked at each other. Suddenly the armadillo ran away, stopped once more, turned its head several times and finally disappeared into the bushes. It dawned on me that in attempting to prove the previous day's lesson to myself, I'd been alternately feeling LOVE and FEAR towards the armadillo, the final outcome of such a state of mind being a vibration of CONFUSION, which confusion had manifested perfectly in the armadillo's behavior!

I walked on, digesting this realization which had "hit me like a ton of bricks." The sun began to peep over the horizon and suddenly all the world seemed at peace. A few birds in the distance began to add their delicate notes to the general harmony of the world orchestra. It dawned on me how flawlessly the Law operates, and how pre-

cisely the moon revolves around the earth, which in turn
revolves around the sun, and so forth ad infinitum; and
how presumptuous man is in assuming that the Laws
which work throughout the entire universe—from the tiny
electrons to the most gigantic stars and planets—somehow
do not apply to him.

Still a little confused, I suddenly became aware of a
rabbit which was sitting in an upright position in a foun-
tain close to the building known as "Pathseeker's Paradise." It seemed as though it had hypnotized itself, and
at first it was unaware of my presence. Remembering my
experience with the armadillo, I suddenly got that "funny" feeling again, and as soon as I did, the rabbit broke
its trance, looked at me, hopped away a few steps, looked
again and disappeared.

"How much more convincing will you need, you dum-
my?" I asked myself. "Well," I answered, "I know they
'picked up' on Confusion, now let's try Love, O.K.?"
I walked over to the steps leading up to the Pathseeker's
Paradise and sat down on the top of the steps. By this
time, the entire sun was visible, and I was feeling what
may be called perfect peace, faith, harmony, and love.
Somehow I felt in tune with the entire Universe, and very
much an integral part of it. I felt very unobtrusive, and
perhaps that is why the two hummingbirds came as close
to me as they did; all I know is that at times they were
within twenty inches of me. Apparently oblivious to my
presence, they allowed me to observe them as they danced
from flower to flower on the bush by which I was sitting.
What marvelous creatures they were, seen from so close
a distance! With what agility did they dance to and fro,
supported by rapidly fluctuating, and fragile, barely visi-

ble wings. For some time, I was totally absorbed in the activity of just looking at them. I convinced myself that feeling what I felt, there was absolutely nothing to fear, and confidently asked for the next experience to prove the point. It came alright. In the form of a spider, crawling on the opposite side of the steps. I observed it as it came closer and closer. My confidence rapidly ebbing away as the distance between us grew shorter, I desperately tried to hold on to the as yet remaining vestiges of my recently acquired faith. Previous conditioning proved too powerful, however.

The spider, still unaware of my presence, stopped a matter of inches below my bermuda shorts, and apparently intended to explore my leg. Fear grabbed hold of me as I muttered: "O.K. Lord, you made your point—not now —please; some other time, alright?" At that moment, the spider's tiny eyes and mine met, and getting the message of Fear immediately, it dropped off the wall of the steps and hastily retreated whence it came.

There were other experiences. One I remember in particular was my "Rescue of the Dragonfly." Having just learned about the ONENESS OF LIFE, I "requested" an experience to prove Life's awareness to me.

It was in the swimming pool at the Ranch, that a dragonfly, floating just beneath the water surface, caught my eye. My first impulse was to leave it be, because it looked dead—and besides—I was a little afraid of it, not knowing whether they could sting or not. Something kept drawing my attention to it, however, while my thoughts continuously reminded me that all Life is One. I decided to gently nudge it towards the edge of the pool. Having accomplished that I carefully lifted it up by its wings and put it on the ground, where it lay silently and motionless. I started to tell myself that I'd really known that it was dead all along—and that I was just an incorrigible sentimentalist who was forever trying to accomplish the impossible—when it—ever so slightly, shook its tail. A strange excitement overwhelmed me as I became thoroughly fascinated with the possibility that Life was still present in this, my tiny fellow creature. Though almost imperceptible at first, it gradually began to tremble all over; first its tail, then its belly, and finally its head. The wings, which had been wet and glued to its body, suddenly stood up. Then it began to sway its head to and fro, caressing it with its forelimbs just like the housefly does it. During the next few minutes, which seemed like an eternity to me, it gained enough strength to stand up and fly away, and that's when a wonderful thing happened. It turned towards me, and, looking straight at me, lifted its right forelimb and waved at me, in the most graceful gesture of thanks I had ever experienced. At that moment, I knew it knew, and we were one. Only vaguely cognizant of the people around the pool, and oblivious to what they might think, I waved back at it, whereupon it flew away.

I cannot describe my feeling at the time other than to say that I was inspired that day to write that "I felt wonderful, for—however insignificant Its form may have appeared to be—I had saved LIFE Itself, and it was good. God smiled, and so did I, and our smiles were One."

Through the rapidly advancing knowledge I acquired in the Conceptherapy classes my awareness of Life increased steadily. I learned that a person who has true Love is all giving, like the sun, which gives freely of its rays, light, and warmth, not caring whether these rays are wasted in space or help to sustain Life on the tiny planet Earth. I realized that all we have has been given to us by our Creator, and that therefore a person who has learned to give all freely has attained to Cosmic Consciousness, for in doing so, he has become like the Creator. I keenly felt the far reaching implications of Gautama's statement, which teaches that "The only curse mankind suffers is the curse of ignorance." I further became aware of the fact that just as the world is a body that is governed by laws, so does man have a body that is governed by laws. I learned about the evolution of human consciousness, and became cognizant of the fact that we're steadily moving towards a NEW CONCEPT of Deity; the old concept having become too limited and illogical for many sound-thinking people. "What the world needs," said Dr. Higdom, one of the Institute's veteran instructors, "is a SCIENCE of the SOUL, which is precisely what we teach in our work, and once this realization dawns fully upon people, CONCEPT-THERAPY will be sought by the entire world." I concur with him completely.

I discovered that in order to *evolve,* we must *involve* first, meaning that we must get to *know ourselves,* which was of course in many ways the essence of Christ's teachings. The beauty of this work was, I felt, that it gave people a blueprint, a map so to speak, whereby they may speed up their own evolution. As an analogy, there are two ways by which we may get to the top of an oak tree: we may climb the tree for a rapid ascent, or we may sit atop an acorn until it grows into a tree. CONCEPT-THERAPY shows us how to climb the tree.

I learned that modern man in essence is the link between stone age and mature (cosmic) man. I also gained a vastly more beautiful conception of the Christ than I had ever had before, and learned that the real purpose of Life is the attainment of the Christ-like spirit; the realization of the one-ness of life—life Itself being a state of becoming, a series of experiences, rather than an end in Itself. I learned how to create an Image about what I wanted to do in life—a Plan—so to speak, and then I learned how to manifest that Image in my physical life, simply by imaging it, concentrating on it, and by putting it to work. With enough faith, I came to know, just about nothing is impossible to man, and an understanding of CONCEPT-THERAPY will without fail supply the required faith.

And so, reader, rather than continuing to tell you of my experiences, I ask you: How would you like to gain unshakeable self-confidence; to rise above the petty annoyances and irritations of everyday life, to be calm in the midst of turmoil? How would you like to overcome and never again be subjected to the effects of jealousy, the nervous tension that goes with being late for an appointment or for work, and gain the ability to detach yourself and your potential stomach-ulcer from the ravaging effects of an argument you can't win? How would you like to increase your awareness of the world around you, be cognizant of the fact that sunflowers always turn their heads toward the sun in the morning, and "follow" it as it turns overhead? And that bees have tiny pockets on their legs, into which they deposit the flower's treasures with tiny brushes? How would you like to be able to SLOW DOWN and be at PEACE?

SLOW ME DOWN, LORD

"Slow me down, Lord! Ease the pounding of my heart by the quieting of my mind.

Steady my hurried pace with a vision of the eternal reach of time.

Give me amidst the confusion of the day, the calmness of the everlasting hills.

Break the tensions of my nerves and muscles with the soothing music of the singing streams that live in my memory.

Help me to know the magical, restoring power of sleep.

Teach me the art of taking minute vacations—of slowing down to look at a flower, to chat with a friend, to pat a dog, to read a few lines from a good book.

Slow me down, Lord, and inspire me to send my roots deep into the soil of Life's enduring values that I may grow towards the stars of my greater destiny."

(Wilford Peterson)

CONCEPT-THERAPY, properly understood, will give you all this and much more.

Chapter Two

"The Story of Creation Retold."

LOVE

How is it that Man wants most that which he understands least? For Love, as distorted in the eyes of Man, is but another illusion. Rather than being the object of any person, place or thing, True Love doth always seek Itself, and must needs be a Love of Life.

Know then that True Love cannot but wound as well as heal as grasped by man's senses, for It lies beyond the senses, and can never be comprehended by them. Therefore only the strong may partake of Its full glory; the weak cannot but be defeated by the illusory hurt it imparts to them.

True Love never binds, but always frees the object of Itself. Love is the beginning and the end, the first breath and the last; it is Truth everlasting, yea, It is the very elixir of Truth drunk from the cup of Life Itself.

Holland, winter of 1968. The air was cold and somewhat misty. I was waiting in front of an open draw bridge underneath which a typically Dutch freight boat was silently passing. As my gaze travelled from the long, narrow boat to the leafless, proud trees lining the canal, many thoughts sought to gain entrance to my mind.

I was on the way to my brother's house. Not having seen Dick for several years, I wondered about how far we'd grown apart. Having emigrated to America and having adopted the American way of life I was acutely aware of my inability to comprehend the Dutch life-style any longer, and felt strange in surroundings which for nearly twenty years had been my home. Though I was very much looking forward to the reunion, I also felt strangely apprehensive about it — and wondered if two "strangers" such as Dick and I would find anything in common to talk about.

My apprehension was unfounded.

Dick, who is a sociologist, and I right away became involved in some rather "deep" discussions. We talked about a great many things, and compared a number of subjects as we respectively saw them from the Dutch and the American point of view. We thoroughly examined and exhausted the present ills of society in general and concluded that since society is in the final analysis a collection of individuals, any change in the situation would have to begin with the individual, which in this particular case meant he and I. Having thus become keenly aware of the necessity to analyze ourselves first, we decided to start at the very beginning, and were thus led into our "treatise" of the story of creation.

We approached that subject in our effort to find "the

meaning of it all," for, since I had recently been divorced, and he was contemplating divorce, being unhappy in his marriage, such meaning seemed all but non-existent in our lives and that of others. In addition to our particular situation, we noted a similar harrowing trend among at least 80% of the marriages we knew of both in America and Holland. We wondered how long people, including ourselves, were going to remain blind to the obvious. The Kinsey report, as well as the current pastime known as "wife-swapping," are but two indications of gigantic social and marital unrest. It appears that all people live on two distinctly separate planes: the self-conscious plane and the social-conscious plane, and that each individual exhibits within himself two completely different — at times diametrically opposed — personalities, in his attempt to play both roles succesfully.

It occurred to us that the conflicts presented in trying to play both roles were sufficient to create many of the psychosomatic diseases so prevalent among society, because so many people are judging in others (social consciousness) the very things they themselves have engaged in or want to engage in privately (self-consciousness — or perhaps this should be called self-unconsciousness). We were cognizant of the existence of a good many people who, if not actually engaging in "extracurricular activities" certainly were laying the foundation for such activity by talking of the desire to do so. The wistfulness of their thinking and the vividness of their imagination was being lent an amount of vehemence and conviction in direct proportion to the recentness and pitch of their latest domestic fight.

Despite all of the idealized pictures presented to us —

we reasoned further — the human animal just was not made to enjoy a life of sexual, mental, and spiritual rekindling and restimulation by the same partner, unless the union was one of soulmates. The fact that wives frequently imagine — if not actually engage in — having sexual relationships with other men (being sexually and emotionally starved by their husbands), and the fact that most married men are often wondering how it would feel to go to bed with "that well-stacked chick down the street" led us to believe that marriage, as a social institution, has turned out to be another mistake. In fact, glancing at the divorce rate, it appeared to be an utter and dismal fiasco. This did not correlate with the statement that God, supposedly a perfect being, sanctified those marriages. It seemed to us that cave men were just wont to simply give in to their sexual desires at will; and that the rule of marriage evolved to keep those men in check who proportionately got more women pregnant than they were capable of producing the amount of work necessary to support the breathing consequences of their acts.

We noticed the same behavior among all classes of society, from the lowest to the highest. Furthermore we noticed how under certain circumstances—such as getting drunk at parties — people would substitute their social-conscious role for the self-conscious role and start acting increasingly more (or less) human according to the amount of alcohol consumed.

We then observed the lack of effect of the moral platitudes liberally sprinkled upon the erring souls by their erring religious leaders, and witnessed the papal hierarchy fail and lose much prestige in its condemnation of "The Pill." People were becoming more independent than ever, to the extent of standing up and questioning the authority of their church. It seemed an outcry for individual FREEDOM of the soul, and in trying to trace the origin of the loss of this freedom, as well as the beginning of human bondage, we decided to start as far back as we could, which was of course the story of Creation as told in Genesis.

We had always wondered as to what had to occur to ensure the future of the human race after Adam and Eve so mysteriously appeared by a logic-defying process which would have us believe that something could be created from nothing. According to the Bible, they had no daughters. Their only offspring was two sons, one of whom killed the other. If we unthinkingly buy this popularly accepted rendition of the story of Creation, we must also accept the fact that all of humanity was begotten from one man without the help of a woman. Yet, according to the law of Genetics at no time in history has it been possible to produce a new member of society without the active participation of the female principle. It therefore appeared to be a logical deduction that the Bible, *exoterically* speaking, did not include all of the facts about the case. Either we are all the products of early incest, or some woman must have been present who was not mentioned in the Bible. If we accept the former, we must assume that we are all begotten from Cain and Eve, his mother, or Cain and another *unmentioned* woman. If we accept the latter, however, we must hypothesize the presence of another family from which this other woman sprang, thus leaving us with the inescapable conclusion that Adam and Eve were not necessarily the first man and woman on earth.

Incongruent also was the fact that an almighty and all-knowing God, who had created Adam and Eve, later could not find them, and had to yell in order to get them to come out of the bushes—which he had also created. It occurred to us that such a description of God was simply the highest representation the writer could offer at that time; his description being limited by the degree to which his particular consciousness had evolved. (Our "unchangeable" God makes quite an evolution Himself throughout the Bible—from the limited conception in "Genesis" to the rather sophisticated one in "Revelations," showing the evolution of human consciousness and comprehension as time went by, and writers were able to formulate their thoughts more clearly as they advance in sophistication.).

To us, the Father of mankind did not behave like a typical father at all. For, after having endowed man with a natural and healthy curiosity, He proceeded to tell him not to eat of the Tree of Knowledge, because he would then know Good and Evil. We could imagine the frustration of poor Adam who, while being driven by his God-given curiosity, was at the same time prohibited from satisfying it! We speculated that, because of this unsatisfied curiosity, emotional conflict may have had its beginning "way back" there. The fact that it was a woman who fell *first* led us to surmise our early writer was a man who believed that women were the original wrong-doers, and that he was endeavoring to keep men aloof and above reproach. In reality, though, he portrayed man as a sniveling little boy who could not hold his own ground, and gave in; presumably in order to keep the love of the woman.

Two very significant questions presented themselves

at this point: one being the question of Free Will versus Predestination, which has plagued religion throughout the centuries; the other question being the true meaning of the Fall. (The question of Free Will verses Predestination will be taken up in a later chapter.)

While religious people have always assumed that the meaning of the Fall was the eating of the apple, it appeared to have a far different meaning to us. The Fall, as we saw it, came about because at that point man separated himself in consciousness from God by questioning God's authority. He thus became self-conscious and fooled himself into thinking he loved Woman more than the Supreme Creator. That is, he began to love the *form* rather than that which was behind the form. In so doing he wandered away from "home" (God-consciousness or Universal consciousness) thus becoming the Prodigal Son. Since then the human race has been lost in this "self" consciousness even though the first commandment, and many supporting Bible passages, leave no room for doubt as to humanity's first obligation. Despite the predominant ignorance of their race, men such as Lao-Tse, Confucius, Buddha, Hermes, Christ, etc., were able to attune themselves with the Infinite and achieve Illumination. Not understanding the process of attainment of the Higher Consciousness (which is nothing more nor less than the process of self-purification through self-analysis; thus placing the attainment of the Higher Consciousness within the reach of EVERYBODY, rather than just a few "chosen individuals") the races that produced these Illuminata worshipped them as gods or prophets. People then, as they do today, seemed to feel that the privilege of the attainment of true knowledge, enlightenment and illumination was reserved for certain special, perhaps holy individuals, and thus robbed themselves of the supreme achievement of life by not even trying. Though more and more people today are beginning to feel that they, too, have the right and privilege to unravel the mysteries of life (and well they should!) many continue to feel that they are not worthy for one reason or another, and content themselves by living a life of "being told what to do" by others. It is this latter group of people that believes the *outer,* or *exoteric* interpretations of the Virgin Birth, Jonah and the Whale, and Prodigal son stories as they are written, and as they are told they should believe them by their religious leaders. It is unfortunate, but these people feel that it is generally safer to follow the advice of those that are supposed to know than to stand up for the courage of their own deep down convictions, which are often in direct conflict with what they are told they should believe. As a result such unfortunate people often feel guilty for having the thoughts and feelings they do, and make themselves miserable in an effort to appease their clergymen and fellow congregationists.

Times are rapidly changing, however, and we have witnessed the emergence of another group of people, which in America alone represents more than one-third of the population. Those people seek to interpret the deeper, *esoteric* meaning and message of those stories, and are generally called agnostics. The esoteric meaning is the *inner one,* and reading the Bible with that purpose in mind we find that its entire message can be expressed in two central statements which occur again and again; namely: That God is one and that man is made in the image and likeness of God. To put it somewhat differently, it attests to the *Oneness* of the Divine Spirit and the Creative Power of Man's Thought. Finding themselves unable to believe in the "angry, jealous," and otherwise limited God-concept, and realizing that they have no official group which speaks for them, they have become seekers in their own right. As such, many of them have come to understand that these stories were purposely written with a double meaning, in order that the *surface, exoteric* meaning might appease those who were incapable of interpreting the *deeper, esoteric* meaning. Many agnostics, several of whom as yet are faithful, though questioning, church-goers have by and large begun to realize that all human beings are Prodigal Sons who will eventually find their way back to the Father's House, which means that with sufficient knowledge we will all become like our Father in Heaven and attain to enlightenment and illumination. This contention is well supported in Bucke's book *"Cosmic Consciousness,"* in which the author clearly depicts the evolution of "Illuminata," and shows that with each age, more such Illuminata come into being. While in earlier times only one such individual would appear once every ten generations or so, we now have several such individuals living among us that have achieved illumination within this time-span.

To achieve such an exalted state of being TRUE KNOWLEDGE must be sought, rather than the knowledge which serves to satisfy selfish motives, and which is kept alive only by virtue of the extent to which it serves to satisfy man's ego. The latter type of knowledge can only serve to ultimately bring man to his knees in humility when he finds out that it was not he, after all, but his Creator, who was and is responsible for man's accomplishments.

Unfortunately though, as man has attained feats which yesteryear seemed wholly in the realm of science fiction, such as extensive space travel, moon landings, etc., he has become more supercilious and complacent by the day. Ignorantly he began to assume that it was he, man himself, who achieved all of those feats, ignoring the fact that as a race he has become unhappier as time went by, filled with complexes, wrong social choices, abject misery, loneliness and a tendency toward self-destruction and suicide. "Of all the species of animal on earth, man often appears to be the dumbest, for his species is the only kind whose members torture, kill and eat each other, build great cities at enormous cost and then blow them to bits, feed hungry children with one hand and drop burning napalm on them with the other, taxing themselves heavily to pay for it all," says Guy Endore of Synanon. Putting it a bit stronger, he continues: "while man has tamed many formerly wild animals, the one animal he has never yet succeeded in taming is himself. And now this untamed beast is in command of the globe, and stuffed with delusional fears, with guilt and suspicion, with undiscriminating love and equally undiscriminating hatred, he is busily stockpiling ammunition enough to blow his kind off the face of the planet, in the crazy belief that there is absolutely no other way to save the *good* mankind from the *evil* mankind than to threaten destruction to *all* mankind."

Being as two-faced as he is, it is no wonder that man, generally speaking, has been unable to attain to true happiness and peace of mind, even though the pursuit of happiness is the primary instinct of every soul. The ultimate happiness, Dick and I agreed, is attained to when the soul has reached its final destination; union with the father, or oneness in consciousness with our Creator.

Yet why, we wondered, have so few people reached this supreme state of consciousness? Did it all begin with the Fall? If so, how did the Illuminata overcome the effects of the Fall? Since obviously they had, it implied that not everybody is subject to the effects of original sin. In fact, the implication once again seemed to be that, given sufficient knowledge, *everybody* is inherently endowed with the *potential* to overcome the effects of the Fall, and all that is needed to achieve illumination is the will and determination to do so.

Having reached that conclusion, we then focussed our attention upon the enigma of the snake. It was the tempter, and supposedly the Devil. Since in reality there is no such thing as a talking snake, our assumption was that it either faded out of existence once its purpose had been served or that it was used by the author as a symbol of some sort.

Furthermore, it puzzled us that the "all-powerful" God did not have enough power to overcome the evil presented by the Devil.

Our conflict intensified when we realized that, if God supposedly created everything, He must have also created the Devil. Consequently, whatever the Devil had to say must have been the Word of God. The Devil, in making his offer to Eve, allowed her freedom of choice. God, on the other hand, in issuing an order did not allow Eve to exercise the free will with which he had endowed her in the first place. Thus we have the irreconcilable situation of a Creator contradicting Himself through his Creations.

The Devil, in snake form, presented Eve with the opportunity to gain the Knowledge of Good and Evil while God, in the form of a voice in the sky, attempted to control her by keeping her in a state of ignorance. (While in the light of the knowledge I have gained in CONCEPT-THERAPY, such reasoning was at best slightly illogical, I am simply reporting my recollection of our conversation as it occurred at the time.) Therefore we felt that the snake handled the situation much like a mature, confident father would, whereas God acted like an insecure and threatened dictator.

Why, of all creatures that could have been used as symbols, was the snake used to do the tempting, we wondered? The snake, to us, was a paradox and as such personified Truth. Both *appear* ugly on the outside yet are beautiful in their essence. If we interpret our Bible correctly (esoterically) we will recognize that to God everything just *is,* being neither good nor evil; while to man, with his limited understanding, the *illusion* of good and bad, ugly and beautiful, etc., is seen as reality. As man instantly recoils in horror at the apparent ugliness of the snake, so does he hastily retreat at the apparent ugliness of Truth. The fangs of the snake seemed perfect symbols for the bite of truth sinking deep into man's inflated ego. Its venom, we felt, could well represent the serum of truth killing man's carnal, self-conscious self, in order that his spiritual self might emerge.

While it presents the Devil in the form of a highly intelligent, powerful and somewhat pleasantly conversing snake, the Book of Genesis portrays God as a jealous, angry father. Dick and I simply could not conceive of a Universal, all-loving God being endowed with such petty human attributes as anger and jealousy. Yet we knew that most people seem to hold both concepts in their mind without ever reflecting on the fact that they are as incompatible as dynamite and fire, never contemplating upon the absurdity of the situation. This brought to mind the fact that a "house divided against itself cannot stand." We felt that many emotional conflicts probably occurred because the mind which holds such conflicting beliefs is divided against itself and as such cannot stand—meaning that it cannot concentrate itself and point itself in one true, undeviating, uncompromising, and all-powerful direction. Instead such a mind, being bewildered and confused, scatters its vital forces dangling to and fro amidst the confusion of its conflicts, never attempting anything new for fear that one of its preconceived ideas might be violated; thus never accomplishing anything far-reaching and worth-while.

Having probed this far, and having reached the conclusion that the Creator endowed us with the faculties of reason and imagination because He intended for us to use and develop them, Dick and I decided to go all the way. "Just for the sake of argument," I said, "let's reverse the characters, and see if the story makes more sense that way. Let's assume that the Devil disguised himself as God, while God expressed Himself through the snake." "You know," said Dick, "it does make more sense that way, because it explains why 'God' acted the way He did." Furthermore, we both agreed, this was a very clever way the true God designed to get us to use and develop our faculties of *reason* and *imagination,* for both faculties certainly were used extensively in arriving at this assumption!

Outside the snow had begun to fall, but we didn't notice it. Stunned by our own "discovery," we simply sat there staring at each other in disbelief. "My God," Dick finally blurted out, "if that is true it'll change the very basis upon which our entire civilization has been built!" Suddenly becoming conscious of his role as a sociologist, he sensed the vast implications of our conclusion with keen awareness, and suggested that before we'd make any attempt to discuss our conversation with anyone, we'd better pursue the matter further in an attempt to reach a different, and a more socially acceptable conclusion. The ensuing conversation lasted several hours, but we finally agreed that we had simply "hit upon" yet another *interpretation* of the Genesis story, and that if we'd spend enough time at it, we'd probably come up with a hundred more and different interpretations. In regard to Biblical history we felt we had no *facts* to go on; just the *speculation* of those who have come and gone before us. As such we concluded that *our particular* interpretation was nothing but pure fantasy, and that the ultimate purpose of our conversation had been the very fruitful attempt to USE and DEVELOP our faculties of reason and imagination. This seemed to be the important thing: the development of our faculties on an individual basis —the attempt to better ourselves by listening to our own conscience and by using our own reason, without being afraid of our own erroneous beliefs — instead of always attempting to fit ourselves in with the creed and dogma of social and religious systems which we could not believe in. Instead of rebelling against such systems, however, we felt that it was far better to ADAPT to them,

while *inwardly* going our own way. After having con-
flicted with social and religious rules, we must always fall
back upon the dictates of our *own* conscience to decide
whether or not we have performed wrong action. Society
may put a man in jail for having committed a crime, but
such action does not necessarily change his inward *thinking*
(which in the final analysis is the realm in which all crime
occurs). He must be given a different belief about himself
and the society in which he lives, preferably in the form
of a meaningful and logical philosophy of life. Chances
are that if he had had a chance to develop his faculties of
reason, imagination, and common sense, he would have
been a useful citizen instead of a criminal.

The term "criminal," we felt, did not necessarily apply
only to the acts of those who commit wrongs against
society, but included the acts of people who commit wrongs
against themselves in the form of emotions such as destructive criticism, fault-finding, gossip, slander, etc. It has
long been known that people who indulge in these negative
emotions are unhappy to the extent that they allow such
emotions to control their thinking. They spread unhappiness, dissatisfaction and negativity into their environment, often affecting innocent children. According to
the author of *"A CRY FROM AFAR,"* there are three
sins (apropos, the term "sin" means nothing more nor
less than "missing the mark," as originated in English
archery) which are more harmful than any other, and
these are gossip, cruelty, and superstition, because they
are sins against Love. "See what gossip does," she says.
"It begins with an evil thought, *which is in itself a crime*
(italics mine). For in everyone and everything there is
good; in everyone and everything there is evil.

Either of these we can strengthen by thinking of it, and in this way we can help or hinder evolution; we can do God's will or we can resist Him. If you think of evil in another, you are at the same time doing three wicked things:

1.   You are filling your mind with evil thoughts instead of good thoughts, and so are adding to the sorrow of the world.

2.   If there is in that man the evil which you think, you are strengthening it and feeding it; and so are making your brother worse instead of better. But generally the evil is not there, and you have only fancied it; and then your wicked thought tempts your brother to do wrong, becoming what you thought of him.

3.   You fill your mind with evil thoughts instead of good; and so you hinder your own growth, and make yourself, for those who can see, an ugly and painful object instead of a beautiful and lovable one.

Not content with having done all this to himself and to his victim, the gossip tries with all his might to make other men partners in his crime. Eagerly he tells them the tale,and they join with him in pouring evil thought upon the poor sufferer. (This explains why there is something to the Voodoo doll mystery after all—namely the overwhelming and often deadly *power of suggestion* as transmitted through thought.) "This goes on day after day, and is not done by one but thousands. Do you begin to see how base, how terrible a sin this is?" she asks her readers, and admonishes them that "you must avoid it altogether."

The thing to be kept in mind is that no one is deliberately unhappy, but that people become unhappy by *un-*

knowingly violating the Laws of Life, and that such violations are mostly brought about because of false ideas, beliefs, and conflicts existing in our minds. Such conflicts are at the same time the result and cause of the ever-present inward battle between our selfish (carnal) nature, and our unselfish (spiritual) one. Our carnal nature is fed by our false beliefs, opinions, and prejudices, while our spiritual nature can subsist only upon the Truth which lies buried deep within our hearts. To reduce the inner tension caused by this conflict, we have the choice of aligning ourselves with our spiritual, unselfish nature, and by so doing we will gain the strength to examine and eliminate most of our age-old beliefs and thus will free ourselves from our mental bondage. In so doing, and by replacing our old beliefs by *facts* which can be obtained from the acquirement of proper knowledge, we will soon be able to perceive the path that leads us into the higher, fourth dimensional consciousness.

Though the truth may hurt our limited, carnal self, it will be as pure nectar for our unlimited, spiritual self, for truth, like our spiritual self, is unchangeable. It's comparable to the law of mathematics, which is unchangeable and can well afford to watch our mistakes; whether we learn to profit by our mistakes by correcting them or continue to make them makes no difference to the law, for being indifferent to such mistakes the law itself is never affected.

"The law itself is never broken, but the individuals who continue to break it are," says Yvonne Graig, instructor of CONCEPT-THERAPY.

Our final conclusion was that we will find happiness and peace of mind in direct proportion to the extent in which we learn to adapt ourselves with the inflexible operation of divine law.

Indeed, there is but one way to gain freedom, and that is by using our divine gift of reason. Reason is the only attribute which separates us from the animal. Knowing this, it makes good sense to assume that our Creator meant for us to use and develop this marvelous gift, for in doing so, we ourselves become creators. We all create our own world, circumstances and environment by thinking them into existence; then acting upon our thoughts in order to manifest them into our physical environment. The Bible states that God has created man in his image and likeness, and the inescapable conclusion in the light of the above is that we must therefore use our reason and learn to THINK in order to become more like God and thus lay claim to our rightful inheritance; that of co-creator with our Father. One prominent psychologist has estimated that 5% of the people think, while 10% of the people think they think, leaving 85% who would rather die than think. Whether his figures are correct or not I do not know; I should rather hope that it is the other way around. In any case, we should learn to use our reason and thinking ability to subject ourselves to rigorous self-analysis. Such analysis can be painful to our carnal, egocentric self, but is as manna from heaven to our spiritual, universal self. In this respect, though, most of us are like the little boy who would rather keep the rotten tooth that hurts him than to have it removed in order to free him from the pain forever. We have a tendency to hang on to our erroneous beliefs to keep from going through the sometimes painful process of removing them and thus be faced with the "unknown," even though the Bible, *esoterically* speaking, distinctly tells us this "unknown" represents freedom, peace of mind, and happiness.

With the use of reason in self-analysis comes true knowledge, and with true knowledge comes faith, which in turn leads us into the attainment of more true knowledge based on fact. The age of knowledge has arrived upon the earth, and those people who yearn for freedom, peace of mind, and happiness must decide now to join the ever-increasing ranks of seekers after truth. The Bible says, "Know the truth, and the truth will set you free." "If a person has any doubt about knowing the truth," states Dr. Fleet, founder of CONCEPT-THERAPY, in *"Basic Principles,"* "then he is not free. And he has the right, therefore, to search for the truth."

More than any other, this is by far the most important decision anyone can ever make.

CHAPTER THREE

"The Rise and Fall of the Nation (s)."

LIFE

The multitude looked upon the Master. As He raised His hand, a silence fell upon them, and He spoke: I will speak to you of Truth, which is like the silver bird whom mortal eyes cannot behold, though now and then It may drop a feather which can be seen only by those sincere souls who are earnestly seeking a better way. Truth is Love, and Love is Life.

Life knows no time; It is never rushed, for time is but another illusion It clothes Itself with. It is only to Man, who has Life but who does not understand It, that time becomes more important than Life Itself. And so he deludes his senses, rushing towards his death, never having lived. The purpose of Life to man is to seek pleasure and to avoid pain. In quiet meditation each day, Life Itself will never fail to provide answers as to how It may be lived to best realize Its own purpose, for Life is Supreme above all, and he who seeks It sincerely, with genuine hunger in his heart, will delve beyond the illusion of the senses, and find Life.

Therefore revere Life with all thy strength, desire, and compassion, and thy soul shall be rewarded with the joy of existence, and will have added unto it all that Life has to offer. Smile with Life, and Life shall smile with Thee, and thy smiles shall be One.

Life is the effort of the soul to free itself from its confining sheaths, in order that it may avail itself of its Divine inheritance.

Nation(s) means Emotion(s). History teaches us that all great nations rise and fall. The Bhagavad Gita states that the emotions must eventually fall, and become subject to the will. While this chapter will explore the symptoms of an oncoming fall of our society as it stands today, it should be read to apply to the fall of the emotions as well. By emotions I mean mostly those destructive emotions over which we seemingly have no control at this time. If we ever are to have peace of mind, we must learn to control emotions such as anger, jealousy, gossip, criticism, etc., instead of allowing them to control us.

All great nations were born — and died — under rebellion. The Roman and Aztec societies serve as two well known examples of this. Our nation isn't any different. Its early beginnings stemmed from rebellion by dissatisfied young men. Curiously, it is this very spirit of rebellion that is branded as antisocial today. It has been said that one of the best ways to get ourselves a reputation as a dangerous citizen today is to go about repeating the very phrases which our founding fathers used in the great struggle for Independence. True ideals have all but left the consciousness of most people, and have been replaced by immaturity and complacency in men. Women were forced to assume a dominant position, in order to compensate for the lack of responsibility shown by the men. The man was thus further pushed into the corner labeled "Mr. Milktoast," and began to spend a great deal of time getting even with his spouse by relating her dominant qualities to his equally hen-pecked friends.

On television, the typical "man" is usually portrayed as a rough-mannered, pushy cowboy, who has a horse for his steady companion. Next in line of importance comes a glass of beer or whiskey, leaving fourth place to a woman. The woman is generally of the saloon girl variety; and our hero has at least one in every city. This sums up Hollywood's contribution to the tacitly accepted image of a "man." The trend which began in cowboy movies is continued in slightly altered form through the portrayal of modern, "sophisticated" and suave man, who is really no man at all. During the course of his adventure-filled day he manages to seduce a number of women, and somehow he never grows tired of it. The fact that the woman is likely to bestow her favors upon a large number of men, rather than confining those favors to our hero, is being happily suppressed by many a male movie-goer, because he needs to hang on to his mental fairy-tale rendition of reality in order to preserve his concept of a "man."

In the meantime, women have gathered a completely different picture of men. Mothers generally don't contribute much to the situation, for quite early in life they begin to teach their daughters how to play certain games with the opposite sex.

This is done to keep the hero interested, and the variety of games played include anything from the numerous variations of the age old "drop the handkerchief" routine to the "be secretive about your feelings" game. An entire volume could easily be written on that subject alone.

Somewhere along the line, the men and women thus conditioned get together and marry. Though they may not be aware of it, it is their subconscious mind that selects their mate. It generally attemps to duplicate childhood conditions, which accounts for the fact that quite often the woman ends up with a husband who is like her father in many ways (though that's the very situation she's tried to avoid) and vice versa. Since both the man and the woman played games so effectively, they fooled themselves and each other into thinking that they were getting their parent's exact opposites.

While according to statistics it is very likely that the above couple will obtain a divorce, we will assume — for the purpose of our illustration — that they decide to remain married. It is easy to perceive the effects this tension-laden environment must have upon the psyche of the child that is born into this "home." For he has the dubious "advantage" of the cumulative effect of centuries of mismatched breeding coupled with a social environment in which the same pattern is present in vastly amplified form.

Because the child cannot be more than the sum total of his genetic equipment and the environment in which he lives, doctors are finding that more and more children are becoming emotionally disturbed earlier and earlier in life as generations evolve. Early schizophrenic behavior can be detected among children with good genetic equipment who have been born in a detrimental environment. One doctor remarked to me: "Children cannot be fooled, and sense hypocrisy in a very real way. Rather than questioning the authority and behavior of their parents — which is often in direct conflict with the child's way of looking at life—the children who have not developed the tough psychic shell required to cope with the situation will retreat into a fantasy world of their own making and thus become schizophrenic."

"The 'normal' children," he further explained, "will find a different way out. Small boys need to feel that their dad is "the greatest guy in the world," and are endlessly outbragging their friends as to the hero qualifications of their dads. It's a plain fact, boys need to be able to look up to their dad as their own personal hero; and a peculiar psychological phenomenon takes place when that image does not measure up to standards. For example: Let us suppose that Mr. Jones comes home after a long day's work. His first act is usually to turn on the TV, as he turns off his family, lamenting that he is too tired to be bothered. His son Stevie is very happy that dad is home, and recognizes no such thing as tiredness, especially when such tiredness interferes with the uninhibited expression of love. In the meantime Stevie's mother commences to relate all the rotten things Stevie did during the day, which she feels need stern masculine discipline. Thus the mother and the child are in competition for the "love" and affection of the father, who in turn has none to give. Occasionally, dad offers a weak defense and expresses the hope that the problem will go away by itself by muttering: "Later, I am watching the news right now." The mood

is set for an uneasy, tension-laden dinner, during which
frustration and pent-up hostilities will quite often reach
the point of no return. An argument ensues. It continues
on beyond dinner time, negative emotions and poor digestion playing hand in hand to secure yet another "victory" for the devil-part of man. Accusations are hurled
back and forth, and the central scape-goat is Stevie,
whom "you should take in hand, because I can't do anything with that kid." Soon both parents are involved in
their fight, forgetting Stevie, who has in turn retreated
into a corner feeling utterly miserable. He has taken
the blame upon himself, and feels that he is the cause
of the argument, and must therefore be a very bad
boy. He sees that his father is acting like a child, and
reasons that it must be because of him that father is
acting this way. In order for dad to remain his hero, he
feels now compelled to do something worse than dad;
thus maintaining the "hero-son" relationship *by comparison*. He pulls mother's prize vase to the floor, which makes
plenty of noise as it breaks to bits. He has now secured the
undivided attention of both parents. The ensuing punishment serves a two-fold purpose: It provides perverted satisfaction to his damaged ego, which reasons that he is the
one who deserves the punishment, and not mother or dad;
and secondly it is an excellent means to get his parents to
stop fighting by having both turn on him.

Stevie will generally become an extremely difficult
child in the early grades of school. The fact that in this
country most first grade teachers are women does not
help matters, for, Stevie reasons, since they've never been
boys they could never understand his problems. In addition,
our educational system is at best confusing to the child,

for though it covers a lot of ground it does not cultivate it. Stevie thus continues to be without an adequate male-model ofter whom he can pattern himself, and turns to TV. Not infrequently Stevie and boys like him will wind up with the label "N.H." or "E.H.," meaning "neurologically or Educationally Handicapped." Once he has secured such a label, he is assured that further effort on his part is quite useless, for he feels he is too stupid anyway. A tragic mistake has been made by many doctors in this country by all too readily labelling certain symptoms which cannot be understood, and then assuming that the condition itself is understood merely because a label has been attached to it," he said. "In America," he went on to say, "eight times as many boys are "neurologically handicapped" as girls, and girls outmature boys until their mid-teens. In Germany the boys outmature the girls, and the explanation seems to be that the "father-image" there is a strong, though often dominant one, and most first grade teachers are males. Thus boys there have a male-model to pattern themselves after."

The same misplaced importance is placed on I.Q. scores. As evidenced in recent experiments, the teacher often classifies a child subconsciously as being dumb, smart or mediocre acording to the number which has been assigned to him in such tests. Generally the teacher never *really* *expects* the child to perform better than his scores indicate he should, and the child responds by performing up to the expectations demanded of him. I.Q. scores are wholly cultural, and as such are not nearly as important as most people feel they are. Certainly we should escape the mistaken notion that an I.Q. score is a rigidly inflexible thing, for far too many people have been detrimentally

influenced by such belief. Analyze yourself in this respect:
How often did you fail to tackle a demanding task, or
refuse to carry out a good idea, simply because you thought
you weren't really smart enough to carry it to completion?
In many ways we all have genius potential; it's just that
individual aptitude is different. The fact that I.Q. scores
are cultural was amply proven by one doctor, who gave a
typically American "peg-in-hole" test to a tribe of African
bushmen. He discovered that by our standards they were
very stupid people, for they failed the test miserably.
Fortunately, he did not draw that conclusion, for in
doing so he would have had to label himself extremely
dense as judged by bushman standards. It so happened
that he himself was the object of much mirth, because
he could not detect the most obvious signs in the bushes
which were interpreted with ease by even the oldest wash-
woman of the tribe. To them, he was undoubtedly a very
stupid fellow. By the same token, Eskimos can distinguish
between several different types of snow, whereas with
luck we may be able to differentiate between two or three.
Many Indians have developed the olfactory sense to such
an extent that they can "smell" snakes; is it to be assumed
that they are smarter than we, or vice versa?

It is easy to see that the process of "labelling" is as
detrimental as it may be convenient, for it has inhibited
the very future of many human beings.

While boys are usually difficult to handle in early childhood, and more so later on, girls often become anti-social
and "anti-parent" during the early teen-age period. Up
until that time they have been able to identify with their
mother to such an extent that rebellion was unnecessary;
but now the differences have become too great. Often-

times girls will become infatuated and marry early just to get away from the family, being determined to make an absolute heaven out of their marriage if for no other reason than to "show her parents." The girl is unaware of the fact that this very attitude — coupled with the automatic response mechanism built into her psychic fabric by early parental example — will be responsible for the deterioration and eventual breakdown of her marriage.

However much we may object, it seems that most of our behavior is compulsive. We have been shaped, molded and conditioned by genetic inheritance and environmental influence in much the same way that Pavlov conditioned his dogs.

THE CALF PATH

One day through the primeval wood
a calf walked home as good calves should;
but made a trail all bent askew,
a crooked trail as calves all do.

Since then three hundred years have fled,
and I infer the calf is dead.
But still he left behind his trail,
and thereby hangs my moral tale.

The trail was taken up next day
by a lone dog that passed that way;
and then a wise bellwether sheep
pursued the trail o'er vale and steep.

And drew the flock behind him, too
as good bellwethers always do.
And from that day, o'er hill and glade,
through these old woods a path was made.

And many men wound in and out,
and dodged and turned and bent about.
And uttered words of righteous wrath
because 'twas such a crooked path.

But still they followed . . . do not laugh
the first migrations of that calf.
This forest path became a lane,
that bent and turned and turned again.

This crooked path became a road,
where many a poor horse with his load
toiled on beneath the burning sun
and traveled some three miles in one.

And thus a century and a half
they trod the footsteps of that calf.
The years passed on in swiftness fleet;
the road became a village street.

And this, before men were aware;
a city's crowded thoroughfare.
And soon the central street was this
of a renowned metropolis.

And men two centuries and a half
trod in the footsteps of that calf.
A hundred thousand men were led
by one calf near three centuries dead.

For men are prone to go it blind
along the calf-paths of the mind
and work away from sun to sun
to do what other men have done.

They follow in the beaten track,
and out and in, and forth and back,
and still their devious course pursue,
to keep the path that others do.

They keep the path a sacred groove
along which all their lives they move.
But how the wise old wood gods laugh
who saw the first primeval calf!

Author Unknown

Undesirable though this picture may be, it is a true one, and we may *prove* it to ourselves by observing and consciously dissecting the habit-patterns we've formed over the years — both as individuals and as a nation. This may range anywhere from observing our own daily habits, such as our first act(s) in the morning. For instance, how do you put your clothes on in the morning? Do you habitually place your left or right leg in your pants first, your left or right arm into your blouse, etc. How many cups of coffee do you drink, how many minutes before work do you leave, how do you back the car out of the garage, what are you thinking about, etc. As for the habit patterns of the nation, we need only look into the fact that our news media have become predominantly sensational, pessimistic and distorted. It is the medium which keeps alive the activity of those rebels who are bent on destruction of our most cherished ideas, by giving them much more publicity than they deserve. Were it not for the attention paid to them by our news-media, the rebel's "cause" would soon die for lack of attention. On the international scene we are constantly being subjected to half-truths, and are being led to believe that somehow we always kill more enemy soldiers than they kill Americans. In much the same way the Arab radios kept informing the public that the Israelites were being crushed by Arabian forces up until the very moment Israel invaded Arabia in the "famous" six days war. Unscrupulous salesmen and advertising executives have hired psychological experts of questionable ethics to devise their advertising campaigns for them, with the result that Americans are beginning to accept the use of all sorts of drugs, tranquilizers, sleeping pills, etc., as a perfectly normal, daily habit — while condemning kids for taking their brand of drugs. Several of these ads *induce* tension; then sell the product that is supposed to relieve that tension. In this way, through legally acceptable means, moral crime has infiltrated the very bulwark of common sense, and has crept into full view of the undiscerning public eye. Cigarette advertisements carry the connotation of romance, courtship and marriage. Constant repetition insures the fact that the message eventually finds its way into the subconscious mind of the listener, who often buys products on impulse (so he thinks), without realizing that he has been persuaded to do so. Advertisements on children's programs are designed to condition them to get mom to buy certain products, the reward for their efforts being a little goodie that comes with the product. To insure the child's attention, various hypnotic tools, such as the fascination phenomenon, rhythm, and others are being used. This explains why kids become "glued" to the set at times, and why they can repeat ads almost verbatim in many instances.

Medical associations, under the label of "public service," stress disease instead of health by publishing lists of symptoms pertaining to cancer, high blood pressure, etc., being apparently oblivious to the fact that these diseases can actually be produced by the agile minds of hypersensitive people, who use these lists as 'guidelines' to materialize their worries. At one time or another we have all met such people. Whenever a list describing a certain disease is published, they go around telling everyone that that is precisely what is ailing them. The great tool of suggestion is thus being used negatively by those who should have public health and welfare foremost in mind. Of course, should people suddenly understand the powerful effects of suggestion, they would set about to change disease-conditions in their life of their own volition; and medical doctors would go out of business. As it stands today, it will probably take a hundred years before such will materialize. Quoting Phase I of conceptology:

"If one would look into the history of medicine and go back to the year 1618, he would recognize that the cure of disease all depended upon the faith of the patient in the remedy which the doctor used. We will quote from the third edition of the reference handbook of the Medical Sciences published by William Wood and Co., New York City:

"It is stated that the first edition of the London Pharmacopoeia, published in 1618, contains a list of 1960 remedies of which 1,028 were simples, 91 animal, 271 vegetable.

Among these were worms, lozenges of dried vipers, foxes' lungs (for asthma), powders of precious stones, oil of bricks, oil of ants, oil of wolves, and butter made in May (for ointments), Vigo's plaster (compounded of viper's flesh, with live frogs and worms), and the celebrated antidote of Mattioli, made up of about 230 ingredients, including the multifarious mithridate and the theriaca Andromachi. The pharmocopoeia of 1650 contains moss from the skull of a person, who had died a violent death, and Gascoynes powder compounded of bezoar, amber, pearls, crabs' eyes, coral, and the blacktops of crab's claws. In the edition of 1667 there was a gratifying absence of the Greek and Arabian names of the medicaments, showing that their influence was disappearing, while such standard remedies as jalap, cinchona bark, burnt alum, digitalis, etc., including Irish whiskey had made their appearance, as had also human urine so highly recommended by Madame de Sevigne. This talented lady also strongly advised viper meat to "temper, purify, and refresh the blood." It was even claimed that Sir Kenelm Digby had poisoned his wife by the too frequent administration of viper's wine, given for cosmetic purposes. Innumerable queer and more or less disgusting remedies appear in all three of the pharmacopoeias; such as horns, hoofs, excreta of animals of all sorts, eggs, viscera, bones, claws, etc. Listed also were "fur, feathers, isinglass, human perspiration, saliva of a fasting man, human placenta, cast-off snake skin, wood lice, swallow's nest, the triangular Wormian bone from the junction of the sagittal and lambdoil sutures of the skull of an executed criminal." etc.

And yet, all these horrible and repulsive doses had their period of success. WHY? If they were successful THEN, why not NOW? They are no longer effective for the simple reason that FAITH in them was lost. Whenever that priceless thing known as FAITH is present in both the DOCTOR and the PATIENT, ANY MATERIAL REMEDY WILL DO. It is, of course, NOT THE REMEDY. IT IS THE FAITH that enables the two to form the COMPOSITE PERSONALITY which must of necessity be formed before a healing can possibly take place.

The same deplorable condition that existed in 1618 is in effect today. Doctors of all schools BELIEVE IN THE MATERIAL REMEDY instead of the POWER WITHIN."

To give another example of the power of suggestion: A few years ago I was reading an account pertaining to the sacrificial rites being used by a superstitious tribe in Africa. The 'offering' in the form of a man is placed in the center of a circle, upon which the tribe begins to dance around him, all of them concentrating upon his death. Invariably the overwhelming power of suggestion, coupled with the victim's expectations and unquestioning belief results in his actual physical death. If the power of suggestion can bring about death, it is easy to see that it can produce many psychosomatic illnesses — cancer being one of them. Because of its apparent lack of public interest — as shown by its initial opposition to medicare programs and its unfounded criticism of many non-medical professions the American Medical Association has been rapidly losing prestige. Notwithstanding the highly-publicized heart-transplants (which in the final analysis have been painfully unsuccessful) it has been sarcastically referred to as the "American murder Association" by a group of dissenters. Deadly mistakes in the name of medicine are made all of the time, but such mistakes are always "hushed-up" very effectively. Much information can be gained on this subject in a book called *"The Intern."* Whenever dedicated individuals brought forth a non-medical form of healing, such as Mesmer did, the local M.D.'s, seeing their income in danger, no doubt— quickly suppressed it. This notwithstanding the fact that the new method *did* bring actual results in many cases where conventional medical treatment had failed repeatedly! Such methods often utilized the power of suggestion as a basic tool. At one time or another, we have all heard about the 'placebo' effect. Briefly, when the effectiveness of a new drug is to be tested, a number of people that could benefit by this drug is divided into two groups. One group is administered the new drug, while the other group receives the placebo in the form of an inert sugar pill. Often the latter group recovered more quickly than the former; the reason for the cure being none other than the power of suggestion, for "it's indeed the thought that heals!" The fact that the group which was administered the new drug sometimes recovered more slowly, and in some cases not at all, seems to indicate that the chemical effects of the drug were actually interfering with the natural healing processes of the body. Throughout history completely different medicines have been used to cure similar diseases with equal success or lack of success. This makes it obvious that the "healing factor" lies not within the medicine used, but rather in the suggestion that accompanies the medication, and the FAITH the patient has in his healer. Jesus once said "Thy FAITH has made thee well" to the woman who touched his garment. Logically, what else could it be? For whenever there is DOUBT on the patient's part that he can get well, none of the available medicine or doctor skill will bring about a cure. Plato once said: "The great error of our day is that in the treatment of the human body physicians separate the soul from the body!" Fortunately, the picture is changing gradually now. Psychosomatic medicine is now teaching that emotional disorder, (which is really soul-sickness) is responsible for a large percentage of all human illness, and young doctors are being trained to treat man's mind and soul as well as his body. Physicians who cannot accept this point of view, must change their viewpoint and method of curing or become extinct.

Politics and corruption are synonymous in the mind of the average American. With so much news pertaining to the unethical behavior of some of our senators one can hardly blame them for their opinion. Frequently we read about political "scandals," in which the politicians involved engage in childish fights and squabbles, and hurl petty accusations at each other—the very thing we punish our children for. The concept of "forgiveness" or tolerance for the other fellow's point of view never seems to enter the picture. Many people seem to be caught in the web of blind political ambition.

A great deal of ambition *seems* necessary to become a politician, but this is in reality not the case. Since "AMBITION" has become almost a deified concept to us, its true meaning has been all but lost. Webster defines it as: "a seeking for preferment; a *consuming desire* to achieve some object or purpose, as to *gain distinction, influence,* etc." (italics mine). It would be far better if the concept "ambition" could be replaced by that of "aspiration", which has a far more noble meaning. Although collective ambition has been largely responsible for America's physical wealth, it has been equally responsible for the nation's spiritual starvation. Through it, man keeps driving himself to his final level of incompetence which he calls his 'goal'. Blind to true values along his journey and all but neglecting the feelings of family and friends, he only discovers a great emptiness of soul when he reaches his destination.

Organized religion has been forced through many changes in order to keep abreast. Some such changes involve drastic alterations of basic policy, implying that heretofore these policies were incorrect. This further suggests that additional changes will be made in the future, from which one can draw the inference that the policies cannot be wholly correct now. In an effort to bolster their dwindling membership, many churches are now advertising their services in newspapers in a business-like spirit of competition. Thus they endeavor to entice people to attend their church, which by some peculiarity of reasoning is the "only true" church among the some 2500 existing religious sects. Christians *say* love one another, but they don't. Churches are failing because they have failed to teach true love. Among the six major religions existing today one basic truth continually recurs; and that is the "golden rule", which seems to have been all but neglected. True Christianity has been turned into bureaucratic 're-ligianity*' and religianity fosters hypocrisy.

As of late, morticians have joined the advertising game.

---

*Term coined to substitute for true religion, which is all but extinct in today's churches.

Since all people must eventually die, what possible purpose could there be in such advertisements other than to snatch as many bodies as possible from the competition? Certainly the business is there in an ever-increasing supply; why, then, plaster huge billboards with "humorous" slogans describing the services of certain cemeteries? The answer points once more towards the all-mighty dollar. For dead bodies equals grieving families with lowered sales resistance equals the sale of expensive floral arrangements and beautiful caskets. Guilt-ridden and unthinking the survivors of the bereaved will often allow the salesman to talk them into going heavily in debt, for after all, he says, nothing is too good for the dearly departed. And who can argue with that statement without at the same time inviting a raging floodtide of conventional opinion to descend upon him? Fortunately, some people have gotten together in the form of clubs; the purpose being the protection of the bereaved against the advances made by over-zealous salesmen at the time when they are most vulnerable. The club members help in the selection of floral arrangements and caskets they feel the bereaved can afford. People who have as yet not made arrangements of this nature would do well to think about the amount of money they will be likely to misspend on a dead person— who could have benefitted so much more while still living. The height of commercial mind-trickery and absurdity takes place when the beautifully hand-crafted and expensive casket is lowered into the ground to rot forever.

People complain about money that's wasted on space programs, but at least that is progress; putting excessive money into the ground where it benefits no one but the mortician (who is now free to dream up additional methods of exchanging our money for his services; having a firm hold upon our thinking *because of custom*), is regress, or retrogression.

Customs dominate our thinking in many other ways. Christmas has all but lost its true significance. Seller is pitted against buyer in a spirit of competition which permeates the otherwise beautiful and peaceful Christmas atmosphere. Instead of practicing good will towards all men, the sellers will advertise their products "to the hilt," not being overly concerned about the practical limitations dictated by the buyers' pocketbook; who in turn go deeply in debt each Christmas season in order to keep up the proverbial "front".

As we continue to live in a more complicated manner, becoming more and more the slave of custom and tradition (rather than their masters), we become increasingly blind to the real truth and simplicity of life. As long as we are led to hate people of certain other nations by our distorted news-media; as long as we condone the savage interpretation of the spirit of competition and all that goes with it as perfectly normal; as long as we are blindly prejudiced against any and all opinions not corresponding with our basic beliefs; as long as we automatically label discerning observers as anti-American; as long as we reflexly react against the color of another man's skin or his religion like a machine instead of a rationally thinking human being, the situation will steadily worsen; for in doing so we are mocking life, and life will pay us our just share through its unfailing law of compensation. The simple truth of the matter is that all life is ONE, and that by bestowing compassion, tolerance and understanding upon our fellow men, especially the 'sinners',

we are doing life a favor, and in so doing we are helping ourselves. We effect the exact opposite result when
we criticize, slander, or otherwise fail to understand our
fellow man. This was, and is, the crux and essence of
Christ's teachings, no matter how much organized religion
has tried to obscure it.

To be able to bestow true mercy upon someone else,
we must first learn to bestow mercy upon ourselves.
To do this, we must learn to clean the psychic
fabric of our own being, which, though by no means impossible, is a very difficult job for most people. For, according to Dr. Fleet's *"Rays of the Dawn,"* "when man
found that he must either give up his evils or be exposed,
the intellect, which has always ministered to artificial
development, gave him the mantle of misrepresentation.
This mantle he has used to its utmost, until today de-
ception and hypocrisy are so universal that their manifold
hues have, consciously and unconsciously, deeply dyed the
whole of human nature. Social relations reek with in-
sincerity and assumption. Religious life has few corners
that are not infested with hypocrisy. In home life lurks
secret disloyalty. Business and political life flaunt their
prostituted honesty, justice and integrity to the four winds
of heaven. There is practically no evil more theoretically
condemned and condoned than dishonesty. It is another
of GREED'S hideous offspring, and an inseparable twin
to injustice. Man dare not effectually attack dishonesty,
for such attack would reach back to its parentage, whose
roots are buried deep in the vitals of civilization. He must
tolerate dishonesty, or yield up greed and shake the institutions built thereon from center to circumference."
It is sobering indeed, to reflect upon the fact that out of

this environment are born those who, under the auspices of man-made law, sit in judgment over the rest of us. It should give us food for thought in future elections, anyway.

As man has wandered further and further from obedience to Divine Laws, he has had to compensate for his folly by devising increasingly complex and contradictory laws of his own. While mostly these laws are designed with good intent; the loopholes they leave to experienced law-breakers more often than not effect a detrimental result.

Driving from California to Texas one day, I noticed signs on the road related to littering. The peculiar fact that struck me was the difference between them as I went from state to state. For instance, in California one can collect $50.00 for bringing a litterbug to the law, (the offender being fined $500.00) in Arizona the fine is a flat $100.00, whereas in New Mexico and Texas there is a range of $10.00 to $200.00.

While the litter question in itself may not be too important, the implications regarding the validity of our laws are, for in this particular instance, the lawmakers in each of these states have interpreted a similar question differently and assigned different punishments to the offense. One then cannot help but wonder how lawmakers can possibly interpret more serious questions correctly, especially those situations where gross moral offenses are interpreted as legally correct, or, on the other hand, where morally justifiable actions are interpreted as legally incorrect.

Indeed, my own experience with the California divorce laws has caused me to wonder many times. Temporary flurries of activity against these laws can be observed among those who are shaken out of their lethargy by coming face to face with the real implications of these laws by their own experiences, but the noise they make is overridden quickly and effectively by the all-encompassing clamor of red tape and inhuman procedures, apparently designed to still the collective voice of conscience forever by attempting to drown it in frustrating legal terminology.

Inefficient though it may be in practical application, it is obvious that we must have legal law, for it serves to put a damper on the activities of the most active catalysts in our ever growing brewing pot of discontent. It is when legal law runs diametrically opposed to the moral law of life that the pot will begin to boil over. For the Law of Life will not be mocked; and a giant catharsis is taking place this very moment. The rebellion of the young people cannot be stopped, however misguided we may feel such rebellion is. Rather than accepting and adapting to the situation, most parents in turn rebel against the youngsters' discontent, overlooking the fact that they are *our* off-spring, and therefore *part* of us, and part of life. The upheaval is inevitable, and has sprung up to tear down an old society in order to build a new and better one, much like an old building must be torn down in order to build a new one in the same location. Unfortunately, many youngsters are in the game just for the destructive aspect of it, and have never given much thought to what they would replace the final outcome of their destruction with. This is precisely where the older members of society could be of invaluable service, for, having experience in these matters, they could lend a helping hand with the rebuilding and re-organization processes. If both

sides could swallow the demon of pride, the final outcome of such working together would be a re-united
country, and who could object to that? After all, the
process of rebellion is by no means foreign to our nature;
in fact, the very existence of our country sprang from it.
Although there must have been plenty of opposition from
the more conservative Americans at that time, we are all
proud of our rebellious forefathers who protested against
the yoke of the British. Yet we attempt to ignore, over-
look, or squelch that same spirit of rebellion to-day. Of
course the present uprising is not just confined to America,
but is taking place in the entire world. News of student
rebellion, embassy attacks, and political upheavals pour
in daily from the far corners of the earth. Can we reason-
ably expect that suddenly all of this should stop, as if
nothing had ever happened? Of course not! What we can
do is to look for, and find, the constructive side of it, the
grand purpose which transcends the life-span of man.
We do this by looking up the facts in our ever-available
history books, where we find that an all-encompassing
rebellion takes place once every two-thousand years or so,
and that the final outcome of such rebellion is always a
new and better world, vastly improved in all details. We
then realize that the last such major rebellion took place
with the advent of the coming of the Christ, almost two-
thousand years ago. Trusting history, the best thing we can
do is to adapt ourselves to the inevitable, have faith that
the Creator knows what He is about, and calmly wait for
a new and better world to emerge out of the present chaos.

The new age being ushered in has been called the
Aquarian age, an age being the approximate 2000 year
period it takes for our solar system to pass through one

sign of the zodiac. Each age takes on the characteristic of the sign in which it resides. The Piscean age was an age in which Christianity was established. When describing the sign of Pisces, two fish swimming in opposite directions are drawn, symbolizing the confusion, sorrow, and tears of the Piscean age. Dr. Fleet states: "Moses ushered in the age of Symbols, Christ ushered in the age of Faith; we now stand on the brink of the age of Knowledge."

Having recently left the Piscean age, we are now embarking upon the Aquarian Age, which will be characterized by an awakening of the Universal Consciousness and an awareness of and love for humanity. It will be an age in which the flourishing of man's spiritual side will enable him to comprehend the spiritual lessons Jesus tried to teach during the Piscean Age. It will be a time when man's expanding consciousness will hasten the expansion of the universe. Unprecedented scientific progress will accompany unprecedented spiritual growth, the culmination of which was described by Jesus when he referred to the beginning of the Aquarian age in these words:

"The wise will then lift up their heads and know
that the redemption of the earth is near."

To be a candidate for active participation in the new, Universal Consciousness Age, we must pass a requirement. A stringent one. The one Jesus referred to time and time again. The one that has been 'overlooked' time and time again. The requirement is: "KNOW THYSELF". And it means just that. No longer can we blame anyone else for our difficulties in life; we must look within ourselves to find the causes. We must look at the fact that we live in an emotional vacuum, our nation having been driven asunder by the very prosperity that was supposed to draw us all together. We must realize the fact that we have wandered far away from our spiritual home, and that in order to return we must discard our inflated ego. We must admit that our 'practical' way of living has turned out to be a dismal failure, as evidenced by the fact that many people no longer dare venture to walk the streets alone at night. When we can idly stand and watch a gang of thugs beat up one of our fellow citizens without as much as lifting a finger, we may rationalize as much as we please; but such rationalizations do not take away the fact that we've become cowards without backbone. We must realize that the average person is swayed by the foregoing influences into adopting a life-style that conforms with social expectations and demands; rather than being enough of an individual to adopt one uniquely his own. Instead of *actors,* we have become *reactors.* We are being tossed to and fro by outside influences, and allow them to control us. We have become dependent upon the very situations that steal the real meaning of life away from us. To "KNOW THYSELF" will mean that we must awaken to the painful fact that we've become the enslaved puppets of our own mistakes and follies, and that no one but we ourselves can clean our psychic closets for us.

Though evil seems to predominate at times, it is not a permanent condition; for evil must eventually retreat before man's faith in himself and in his fellow human beings, which he can only gain by throwing off the shackles of erroneous social conceptions.

> "Fear knocked on the door,
>   Faith got up and answered,
>   There was no one there."

Yes, in order to gain Freedom, we must learn to be *individuals*. We must learn to be *actors,* rather than *reactors*. I am reminded of a story I read in this respect: A reverend and his friend daily walked by a newspaperstand, and as part of the daily routine the reverend purchased a newspaper from the vendor. While the reverend would always greet the vendor in a very pleasant manner, the latter returned his greetings in most inhospitable terms. Noting the lack of manners and negative behavior of the vendor, the reverend's friend remarked one day: "I don't understand why you never get mad at that guy, and tell him to mind his manners." Whereupon the reverend remarked: "That would be silly; why should I allow him to influence my behavior?" While most people think in terms of the friend, they fail to see that by so doing they are *reactors,* and allow other people's feelings to disturb their own state of mind. The reverend, by being an *actor,* is teaching us a very valuable lesson. We must plot our own course in life and determine for ourselves what we will believe. We must become like the ocean bed — while many emotional rivers flow into our psychic ocean, the bed itself is never moved, and remains undisturbed as it watches the rivers come and go, partaking only of those it chooses. We must resolve to get the facts for ourselves; to be no longer influenced by theories or fantasies. We must realize that follies do exist, and have much greater influence upon our own lives than we are willing to admit. Just because an entire nation holds a certain belief or follows a certain course the essence of which it knows little or nothing about does not mean that its chosen course should be accepted as the right one. After all, the entire world was once in error in believing that our planet was flat, until Galileo came along and proved otherwise. Today the whole world has been deeply influenced by that one man who dared to be an individual and challenge prevailing opinion.

So dare to be an individual, one who refuses to react to provocation, with definiteness of purpose and a steel will welded by iron self-discipline, tempered by true compassion, joy of living and an all-encompassing love for life and fellow man; thus setting your foot upon the path of attainment that will lead you into the next dimension of freedom.

According to all the available literature upon the subject (Edgar Cayce's statements for one), we really have no choice, for we must all reach the FOURTH DIMENSION sooner or later. Having passed the state of simple, animal consciousness, we are now nearing the completion of the self-consciousness stage, and are being prepared to embark upon the state of cosmic consciousness. It stands to reason that the sooner we embark upon this most worthwhile of journeys, the sooner we shall reach our destination. It is then when we will discover the answers to the mysteries of Life; when the crumbling barriers of self-consciousness will yield up their final secrets to our ever-growing determination. It is then that we'll discover that rather than being pinpoints of life in a dead universe, that as long as we remain self-conscious we are really specks of relative death in a vibrant and living cosmos. It is then also that we'll discover that man is the very highest of creation, and is destined to become a co-creator with the Supreme Being.

Chapter Four

"This — The Beginning of Cosmic Day."

RELIGION

For those Souls who do not yet understand the higher Laws of Life, Religion is one of Life's tools to gather Its sheep unto Itself.

Though the thinker may wonder, and the lover be confused, and the true practice of Religion is all but naught, Its purpose remains forever the same, undisturbed by the passion of man.

Take care to practice religion, and not religianity, for religianity fosters hyprocrisy.

Therefore, if you would serve life, and as yet do not understand the realms which lie beyond Religion, serve your faith, not by the letter, but by deed; not by word of mouth, but by action, and the day shall surely come that you be lifted in understanding. Yea, you shall gain Wisdom, and be Free.

To any discerning observer, life is a definite process of evolution. While science and religion have been at odds for many centuries in this respect, they have only disagreed on labels — never in essence. In attempting to explain the Beginning, science presupposes the basic building block of the universe to be the electron, and states as its universal law that "Energy Is". Religion, on the other hand, traces the beginning to the existence of a Master Mind labeled "God", and states as its basic law that "God Is." Being the two major sources of all of our knowledge, science and religion have confused mankind since creation, especially in the realm of metaphysical conceptology (says Dr. Fleet: "Between the agnosticism of science, and the dogmatism of religion, true knowledge has been crucified.") This has been so because apparently neither understands that that which science calls "energy," and what religion calls "God," in reality represents one and the same thing: namely the "Unknowable." To illustrate it in simple mathematical terms:

$$\text{If } x \text{ is equal to } y,$$
$$\text{and } y \text{ is equal to } z,$$

then it follows   that x is equal to z.

Letting 'energy' represent 'x' and 'God' represent 'y' and the 'unknowable' 'z', we can readily see that Energy $(x)=$ the Unknowable $(z)=$ God (y); and deduct that 'God' and 'Energy' are but representative labels in an attempt to explain one and the same thing, namely the 'Unknowable.'

"However many theories may exist as to the beginning," explains Concept-Therapy, "we cannot but start with an unknown in our attempt to trace the evolutionary process. The thing to be remembered is that Man, with finite consciousness, demands a beginning and a boundary, though this is not necessarily a logical assumption." We thus assume that in the beginning there was a sea of spirit, and it filled all space. "It was static, yet ever moving; content, aware of itself, a giant resting on the bottom of its thought, contemplating itself. Then it began to move, withdrawing into itself until all space was empty, and that which had filled it was now shining from its center in the form of a restless, seething mind. This was the individuality of the Spirit; this was 'Energy,' or 'God.' Spirit desired to express itself, so it projected from itself the cosmos and souls. The cosmos was built in very logical and step by step fashion, utilizing the tools and laws which man has labeled arithmetic, music, and geometry, manifesting in system, harmony, and balance," (From "There is A River.") The Building blocks were all of the same material, namely the "life-essence," or electrons. It was a power sent out from the Unknowable which by changing the length of its wave and the rate of its vibration became a pattern for different forms, substances and movements. As in music certain notes are arranged to create certain chords and melodies, the Unknowable arranged Its building blocks of electrons and atoms into certain forms and thus created the world of molecules, compounds and minerals. While the electrons possessed individual consciousness, they had to dispense with such consciousness in order to become a part of the overall consciousness of the more highly complex molecules, compounds, and minerals.

The reason for the building process can only be surmised

as the desire of the 'Unknowable' to express Itself in more abundance through Its Creations. The fact that consciousness, or 'life force', is present in electrons cannot be denied, but it is present in very limited form which man calls positive and negative electrical charge. For reasons unknown to man, certain electrons attract each other, while others repel, and the electrons seem to 'know' which to attract and which to repel!

The life force kept right on building its mineral world into perfection, in order to eventually prepare it for a yet higher form of expression — that of the vegetable kingdom.

In preparing for the "changeover," it created a substance which had the attributes of both the mineral and vegetable kingdoms, namely the diatom. The word 'changeover' is really a misnomer, for it implies a drastic change in state of being from that of the mineral kingdom to that of the vegetable kingdom. In reality it was but another smooth transition; an evolution from a lower form of expression to a higher one; from a simple to a more complex expression of the Spirit. Utilizing the mineral world for growth and nourishment of the vegetable world, the Spirit was now free to express Itself in undifferentiated growth and heretofore unmatched beauty. The many varieties of plants were able to express the Divine Consciousness to a much higher degree than had heretofore been possible. A rudimentary 'brain' or guidance mechanism took its seat of consciousness right within the root-tip of the plant, its main function being the guidance of the root towards sources of nourishment. Almost everyone has had experience with the latter, i.e.: Plants have been observed to grow under the most adverse of conditions, the 'consciousness within' leading them to find cracks in concrete pavement through which to grow; in other instances plants have been known to crack water ducts in an effort to find water, to the dismay of many a gardener. Recent scientific experiments have further borne out and elaborated upon the existence of this consciousness: One experimenter boiled shrimp in the presence of a plant. He noted that each time he put a live shrimp into the boiling water, the plant would "cringe." As he proceeded, the plant reacted less and less, as if to say, "well, I might as well stop reacting and *adapt* to the situation, for it looks as though he's going to go right on killing them anyway!" In another experiment one man out of a group was elected as the 'plant-molester.' He went into the room, where he proceeded to severely cut, bruise and damage the plant there. The plant was then given ample time (about six weeks) to recover, upon which the men entered the room one by one. While the plant remained passive in the presence of the other men, it reacted immediately when its original molester entered, showing that it had, in addition to immediate awareness, something akin to memory! Many truly amazing experiments have been performed in this respect, and the reader is referred to the scientific works upon this subject. The more highly evolved a plant becomes, the more it becomes susceptible to certain nervous disorders as we find them in the human kingdom. Some plants are exceedingly sensitive, and fold their leaves immediately upon being touched. This would also seem to explain the 'green thumb' phenomenon, for plants apparently are very sensitive to love and harmony, and almost always grow better when such attributes are present in abundance.

In the meantime the Creator of Life Force was moving onward towards a better expression of Itself, preparing Its world for Its next higher creation: that of the animal kingdom. While the vegetable kingdom had started with very simple plants and vegetables, its final stages produced plants with many animal-like qualities. According to the Concept-Therapy text, the foremost of these appears to be a plant known as the 'Devil's Noose, found at the banks of Lake Nicaragua. It is a vicious, flesh eating plant which traps small animals such as rabbits, squirrels, dogs, etc. It 'knows what it wants', for, having eaten the flesh, it rejects the fur and bones, etc. Further life-like expression can be observed in the 'traveling seeds' of certain plants, which, having dislodged from the mother plant, are carried along the river stream towards their future habitat. At the 'chosen spot' they work their way to shore by means of tiny projecting filaments, which they use to project themselves. "So curiously life-like are their movements," said a botanist in explaining the behavior of these 'swimming' seeds, "that it is almost impossible to believe that these tiny objects, making good progress through the water, are really seeds and not insects."

THE SPIRIT OF GOD MOVED UPON THE FACE OF THE WATERS:

Having completed the vegetable kingdom, the Creator then said, according to Genesis: "let the waters bring forth abundantly the moving creatures that have life, and let the fowl fly above the earth in the open firmament of heaven." This rendition is the accepted rendition of the theologists, who teach us that the first, *animated, MOVING* life began in the sea, and then later appeared on land. Regarding this very important stage of creation, science is once again in agreement with theology, for it also teaches us that *animated, MOVING* life evolved from the sea to the land: "CONSCIOUSNESS in animal life varies from the first faint glimmering in the single cell in the slime of the ocean bed (the monerons, then the protozoa, then the amoeba, etc.) to full dawn in the highest form of animal life like the horse, the dog, the elephant, etc." (page 8, CONCEPT-THERAPY).

"Details were gradually perfected in orderly, logical, and awe-inspiring fashion, from the generalization of the first simple one-celled creature called the moneron, which was capable of absorbing food through all of its parts—to the more complex organisms, in which specialized organs have been added for the purpose of performing specific services. Thus the digestive tract was specifically designed to perform functions relating to nutrition, digestion, and elimination. In like manner the circulatory, nervous, glandular, muscular and reproductive systems evolved and were assigned tasks relating to their domain of activity only. The brain evolved as the control mechanism which kept all of these systems in such balance as to promote the ultimate welfare of the entire organism." (Concept-Therapy).

The greatest single attribute present in animal life that differentiated it from plant life was that of *movement*. The animals were free to move about from place to place in seeking and securing food. Having *freed* them from the one-location existence of the plant world, the Creator thus added another attribute towards a better, freer, and more perfect expression of Itself. The Creator kept full control of the situation by guiding the animal's behavior through the mechanism known as INSTINCT. The animal cannot think for itself in most instances, but is controlled at all times by subconscious, universal mind. The control mechanism being utilized by the Creator appears to be that of vibration. Animals are extremely sensitive to vibration, and seem to "sense" whether a person, situation, or thing is friendly or hostile towards them. A dog will snarl and bare its teeth at a dog-hater, and be perfectly passive or friendly towards an animal lover, though neither one of these people show any outward sign of their inner feelings. Likewise, we may observe how a school of fish will suddenly turn about and swim in another direction as a result of some vibratory disturbance in the water. It seems as though the entire school, though composed of many individuals, has become as ONE in its response to the vibratory stimulus.

Much can be learned by observing the animal world. Take for instance, the world of ants. Intelligent though they may be, the ants appear to be totally unconscious of the human world, even though they are living in it; much in the same way that we humans are living in God's world, yet are virtually unaware of it. Watching the definite goal-directed purpose and expression of life in the ant colony, we cannot help but marvel at its supreme intelligence. In testing the colony's goal-directed response, we may take an object such as a small stone, and put it near the entrance of the colony. Without fail, the ants seem to know what to do. A sufficient number of ants is "summoned" to remove the foreign object — this having become the most important task for the moment. In the meantime, the other ants carry on life's processes as usual. We may do other experiments, such as putting bits of cheese, ham, candy, etc., within the range of the colony. We will find that soon the foods are being sorted out according to certain preference, some being carried in for immediate consumption, others being stored for future usage, yet others being discarded. Every housewife has had experience in watching the Supreme Intelligence at work in the form of a long, narrow trail of ants marching on her kitchen table. Somehow, the tiny creatures had 'homed-in' on a few forgotten crumbs of sugar.

Many more examples can be quoted, such as the annual trek birds undertake. Leaving at a specific day and hour, they arrive unwaveringly at a precise moment in time at their exact destination. Man himself would be utterly lost without navigational instruments, yet birds arrive without fail at their destination without consulting charts, weather conditions, instruments, and so on. One species of birds leaves its nest upon having mated, later to have the offspring of its youngsters return to that nest, even though they've never been there before!

The same feats of instinct can be observed among the water creatures. Just about everyone is familiar with the annual salmon journey. Having hatched in the river, the salmon swims out to the sea and spends its life there, upon which it returns to its original spawning place to hatch and die. At the time of return, the Supreme Intelligence directs bears to the shallow spots in the river, who proceed to catch a portion of the tired, returning fish in leisurely fashion. Apparently the continuation of life is extremely important to the Creator, however, for a sufficiently large number of salmon is impelled to always 'make it', starting the new cycle, and discarding the old. Another example is the international brotherhood of eels convening in the Caribbean Sea for their "anual convention" after which they return to the 'home' of their parents in a very remote corner of the world.

It is as though all animals were held by invisible strings of intelligence and know-how, the species being maneuvered to where it will do them the most good; the lower species often having to give up their life in order to sustain the higher. These examples are reminders that in all creation Awareness Is, and that each new form of Life is Awareness demonstrating Itself in ever-increasing complexity. The obvious lesson to be learned from this is that man's most important activity is to become aware. Aware of what? Aware of his source.

"Up to this point, all forms of life, from the lowest to the highest have been guided by the force known as IN-STINCT." (Concept-Therapy, page 10) "Originally CONSCIOUSNESS started with nothing but the single attribute of ENERGY. Traveling through eons of time, it added attribute upon attribute to model after model, ever increasing in complexity on the one hand, yet remaining simple and uncomplicated on the other. Traversing beyond INSTINCT, the Creator now added the attribute of REASON. The FORM He chose through which to express this attribute became a creature known as MAN." Having passed through the Electronic, Mineral, Vegetable, and Animal phases of Creation, we now entered upon the Human phase. This corresponds with the Fifth Day of Creation in the Bible, the Sixth and Seventh yet to be completed.

"In bestowing REASON upon Man, the Creator now made a drastic, and most significant, change in its mode of expression. While heretofore only one Consciousness had held undisputed sway, this Consciousness now became divided into two distinct entities, namely the original, Universal Consciousness of the Creator, and the limited, Self-Consciousness of Man. The latter is the consciousness which enables man to see himself as a being separate from his fellow man (often much to his detriment); to say of himself "I am," and identify himself as the thinker apart from his thoughts, the feeler apart from the feelings, and the actor apart from the action." (Concept-Therapy, page 10) In becoming increasingly self-conscious, man separated himself more and more from the general trend of universal consciousness. This too, however, was in the Creator's plan, for in so doing man was enabled to develop his self-conscious faculty to the utmost. In pursuing and satiating his own interests long enough, man will eventually come to the conclusion that no lasting happiness can be gained this way. It is in the wake of such deeply felt realization that he will humbly decide to try anything to get out of his misery. It is then that he will become aware of the needs of other people around him. It is then when he will place his faltering steps upon the road which will lead him back into Spiritual Consciousness. It is then when he is on his way towards becoming a "more perfect vehicle for perfect spiritual expression." And it is then that the Creator can use him towards the fulfillment and perfection of His Idea.

The tremendous significance of this may scarcely hit home with many people, yet it is the true meaning of the Biblical statement that: "Man is created in the image of God"; meaning that he has been destined to become a co-creator with the Supreme Being. Many people have mis-understood that statement to mean that man's *physical* appearance must have been created in God's image, and that therefore God must look like a man. This is erroneous thinking, considering the fact that man's body is not the man at all, but is the vehicle he occupies during his brief stay on earth. Man is SOUL, and SOUL is eternal, being part of the Creative Force or Spirit. Man creates himself by the thoughts he thinks, and by the actions he performs. Negative thinkers create ill-health conditions in their life by constantly concentrating upon such conditions through excessive and needless worry.

"Behold, that which I feared has come upon me."

Positive thinkers, on the other hand, create for themselves a pleasant, healthful atmosphere, and enjoy life from that vantage-point.

Through his thoughts, man creates himself, the ideal object of such creation being perfection — which is necessary in order to enter the Fourth Dimension. This is the true significance of Christ's statement: "Be ye therefore perfect, even as your father in heaven is perfect." Taken one step at a time, such perfection can be reached almost effortlessly, as long as the faith and the desire to do so are present, and any tendency to doubt is discarded immediately.

Evolution has been the long-sought missing link — the 'go-between' that could reconcile religion and science. While many people still object to and repress the overwhelming evidence in favor of evolution, it seems that both man and monkey evolved from some common ancestor; the ape occupying one limb of the ancestral tree, and man the other. As stated in the Concept-Therapy text, "Huxley has pointed out that the brain structure of man as compared with the chimpanzee shows but slight difference as compared to the differences between that of the chimpanzee and that of the lemur." According to M. Sarich, assistant professor of anthropology at the University of California, Berkeley: "The hemoglobin sequence shows that man and the ape are as similar as the donkey and the horse." In addition, biology teaches us that most fetuses, from the frog fetus to the human fetus look exactly alike in the early stages of development. Only time can tell which is which. Does that mean that man evolved directly from the ape? In other words, were a set of ape parents suddenly confronted with a human baby? . . . No!

While the 1970 Ford may have most of the attributes of the 1930 Ford — such an engine, wheels, tires, lights, etc. — and has evolved to be a much better car than the early Ford, it did *not* evolve from, nor was it born directly through, the 1924 Ford. When you comprehend the analogy, the "mystery" of evolution will no longer be a "mystery." The main difference is the *idea* of the creators of the model, this idea being perfected in detail — and improving steadily — as models were produced and tested for flaws. Such "practice" is necessary for subsequent manifestations to materialize in better and better form, ever improving towards the goal of perfection. This explains why the human kingdom as yet is by and large in such an imperfect state of being, and why such large differences exist between its members. For while some of us still live as stone age man did, others have reached the moon. Most of us will agree that the latter group has attained to a higher state of perfection than the former at this time. The very term "evolution" implies a 'state of becoming' something better than what we are. This being the case, it stands to reason that we will continue to evolve until we've reached the goal of perfection, for what else is there to evolve to?

When REASON appeared, it became necessary for man to remove himself in consciousness from his Creator, in order to develop his newly acquired faculty on his own. Doing extremely well in some areas, he has failed miserably in others. For while he has used his reason to *survive* in most admirable fashion, he has not yet learned to use it to teach him how to *live*. From all appearances, however, he is now taking the first steps towards such usage. As the faculty of reason develops sufficiently, other faculties come into being. According to CONCEPT-THERAPY, these are the faculties of imagination, perception, and intuition. Becoming sufficiently proficient in their use, man will suddenly realize that he has been the prodigal son all along. In the wake of such realization, he will begin his return journey towards his Divine Home, where his Father is waiting for him. The "homing device," though consciously suppressed, has always been, and will always be, man's main driving force towards his inevitable goal. Of the several basic urges buried deep within his subconscious fabric, the desire to return to Heaven is by far the most powerful. This explains why man is basically a religious being, as proven by the fact that throughout the centuries he has worshipped his idea of a supreme Being, whether that was the fire god or the holy trinity.

"Thus the plan for the Soul was a cycle or series of cycles of experiences, unlimited in scope and duration, in which man could come to know Creation in all its aspects, at the discretion of his Will. The cycle is to be completed when man's will is no longer different from the thought and will of the Supreme Being, or God. Man's consciousness will then merge with its spiritual consciousness of identity with the Creator, upon which the Soul will have returned to its source." ("There Is A River")

While in this state, the soul will retain its consciousness of a separate individuality and will be aware of its own free will. It now acts as a part of the Supreme Life Force, or God, not diverting the mind force because it is in agreement with the action towards which this force is directed. (Most people are unhappy, nervous, and ill because consciously or unconsciously they live their life in opposition to the trend of the main Life-Force. Consequently they will be much happier and healthier if they learn to align themselves with this basic Life-Force. The methods by which this may be accomplished will be explained in a later chapter). Until this state is reached the soul cannot be God's co-creator in the true sense of the word.

"On the surface," states Dr. Fleet, "the idea that a return to God means a loss of individuality may be paradoxical to the thinker, since supposedly God is aware of everything that happens and must therefore be aware of the consciousness of each individual." This is explained by the fact that the return of the soul is simply the return of the image to that which imagined it, the returned soul becoming aware of itself not only as a part of God, but as a part of every other soul, and everything. What is lost is the ego—the desire to do other than the will of God. When man has finally cleansed himself enough to return to his Creator, the ego is voluntarily relinquished; and this is the true significance of the crucifixion symbology.

In summary, it can be seen that all Creation is a process of Evolution. Until reason appeared on the scene, all was well, and proceeded under the direction and control of one Director only. The consciousness in electrons, minerals, and plants was the same as the consciousness and Will of the Creator, and therefore could not act contrary to it. The same is true for the instinct in the animal world. It, too, could not interfere with the direction of Universal Consciousness, and therefore could not produce adverse conditions such as psychosomatic diseases and the like. So far, the Creator *originated* the ideas, and his creations *executed* them without question. This they did because they had no choice or reason, for up until the creation of man the Creator did all the reasoning. Man, being given the power of conscious choice, frequently made wrong use of his reason. With his power to originate and execute ideas contrary to the Universal Will, he has managed to create ill-health conditions in the form of psychosomatic diseases which heretofore had not existed. "For all his reason," says the Concept-Therapy text, "he has lived in a pit of ignorance." The depth of the pit he occupied was in direct proportion to the extent of his ignorance, which in turn was in direct proportion to the size of his ego. Quoting the Concept-Therapy text: "For millions of years he has been climbing up out of this pit towards a greater perfection. Generations lived and ceased to exist. Man steadily advanced while other forms of life remained stationary. The worm and cockroach are virtually the same today as they were millions of years ago. Today's bats are but diminutive representatives of their large ancestors. Even the apes, after advancing far, seemed to forget what it was all about, and contented themselves with an aimless life among the tree tops. But man advanced, and restless and dissatisfied, continued to struggle upwards. Finally a large section of mankind reached the mouth of the pit of ignorance. Man still has to climb to reach the stars. Though it may take him a long time to reach his final kingdom in the heavens, his constant restlessness and ceaseless ambition are evidence of his determination to continue climbing to the limit of his possibilities. He has inherited memories from his stay in the pit—stored in his subconscious mind and therefore not readily available to him. He is ashamed of his past and therefore represses it from conscious thought. Not at all proud of the feelings and actions of his forefathers, he has tried to blot them out of his existence. He fails to realize how much they control his life through the genetic equipment he has inherited from them. By the same token he fails to realize the extent to which they can be helpful to him if he'd but learn to still his mind and listen to the inclinations coming from the depths of his being."

"The mouth of the pit of ignorance is the "threshold of consciousness." The barrier with which man has attempted to close the pit is the "psychic censor." Below the barrier is the sub-conscious mind, above it is the conscious mind. Man has purposely willed (consciously) to remain ignorant of the life below the barrier. He has done this because he is ashamed of the thoughts, feelings, and inclinations he gets from "down there," and because of his shame, he remains ignorant. At night, however, things are different. For while he may resist the message from his ancestors by blotting them out when he is awake and conscious, he cannot prevent them from coming through in the form of dreams while he is asleep. At such times he is often plagued with thoughts and feelings he dares not speak of—save perhaps to his psychiatrist. Only in primitive men there was no repression. Their emotions were harmless as long as they were understood. It is ignorance of the effects of such repression that has caused all of the misery of the human race. It was the deliberate blocking of the mouth of the pit that has produced all of the complexes, neurasthenia, hysterias, anxieties, phobias, and inferiority complexes. The more man knows about his past, the better able he will be to understand his present and prepare intelligently for his future—the less his ignorance, the greater his health and happiness."

Further quoting Concept-Therapy:

"Thus, by better understanding himself, man can become more capable of living a normal life. Problems become challenges, none of them being unconquerable. The problems his ancestors solved he no longer has to face, but problems will come his way, for that is the way the Creator makes men grow. All of his life is simply a reproduction of the composite life of his ancestors, and in that knowledge—when properly understood—lies the cure of most of his ills. Now, he no longer has to depend upon himself alone in the struggle of life, but he has the constant assistance of millions of ancestral helpers who have travelled the path before him, if only he will allow them to cross the threshold of consciousness. With the full utilization of his gift of REASON, man can then learn the natural Laws that govern the Universe, as well as the Laws that govern his Body, Mind, and Soul. By obedience to these Laws, he will obtain health, happiness, and success. He becomes a *real man*. He has for a mate a *real woman*, who has also lifted the lid that has kept her in ignorance and thus has learned to act normally."

The process of Evolution is as active today as it has ever been, and it is presumptuous to assume that it will stop with man. On the contrary, it will continue right on, projecting man into the next higher state of COSMIC BEING, in much the same way that some of the most highly evolved apes could have been projected into the state of HUMAN BEING. It will, through the processes of natural elimination, such as pestilence, disease and war, discard those species of men who steadfastly refuse to align themselves with the inevitable. If this makes good sense to you, then so will The Laws as they are thought in CONCEPT-THERAPY, which are summarized as follows: First we have the Seven Universal Laws or Hermetic Principles, all of which operate under the one great Law of: "ENERGY IS:" and they are:

1. The Law of Perpetual Transmutation of Radiant Energy

2. The Law of Relativity

3. The Law of Vibration

4. The Law of Polarity

5. The Law of Rhythm

6. The Law of Cause and Effect

7. The Law of Gender

In briefly explaining these Universal Laws, I will quote certain segments given in the CONCEPT-THERAPY text:

1. THE LAW OF PERPETUAL TRANSMUTATION OF RADIANT ENERGY: This Law explains the truth that everything in the material universe; including all that we see, hear, smell, taste, feel, and experience is simply a manifestation of different forms of Energy. The Law explains the true nature of FORCE, POWER, and MATTER, and why each in its turn can be controlled by Radiant Energy—such as the Energy given off by our thoughts. It furthermore explains all phenomena that occur under the "Mind Over Matter" category.

2. THE LAW OF RELATIVITY: Under this Law we find that all things are relative. All Laws are related to each other—correspond with each other. There is no big nor little, fast or slow—save by comparison. An understanding of this Law will give you the means of solving many of the secrets of Nature that seem paradoxical.

3. THE LAW OF VIBRATION: Under this Law we find that all things are in constant motion. All things vibrate; nothing rests. Energy is manifested in all varying degrees of vibration. Rates of vibration are now known as frequencies. The higher the frequency, the more potent it becomes. The X-rays and gamma rays, because of their high frequency, can penetrate solids. Interestingly, this Law explains why thought waves are so effective and powerful, for having the highest known frequency (much higher yet than X-rays and gamma rays) they can pene-

trate anything and everything provided one knows how to focus and direct them properly. Another very interesting point is that the much-talked of Fourth Dimension is nothing more nor less than the Dimension of Vibration.

4. THE LAW OF POLARITY: Everything in the Universe has its pair of opposites. All opposites are identical in nature and differ only in degree. There is no absolute cold, and no absolute heat, but heat and cold are really the two extremes of the same thing, with many varying degrees of temperature between them, just like the North and South poles are nothing but opposite aspects of the Earth, positive and negative, differing only in potential and direction. The Law of Polarity explains all of the apparent conflicts of feelings and paradoxes in nature as no other Law will. Understanding this Law enables you to change your own polarity from positive to negative, and vice versa. Applying it, you may change your mental state from a negative, destructive and unhappy mood to a positive, constructive and happy one.

5. THE LAW OF RHYTHM: The Law of Rhythm embodies the truth that everything is moving to and from, flowing in and out, swinging backward and forward, has a high and low tide. It can be observed at work in the rising and setting of the sun and moon, the ebb and flow of the tides, the coming and going of the seasons, the rhythmic swing of consciousness and unconsciousness. It manifests in the physical states of the human body even unto the functioning of its organs. A thorough understanding of this Law not only gives you a better insight

into the operation and functions of the organs of the human body, but also gives you keen insight into the function of your mind, as well as the minds of others.

6. THE LAW OF CAUSE AND EFFECT: Every cause has its effect; every effect, its cause. There is no such thing as chance, for everything happens according to Law. It is impossible for the human mind to conceive of starting a new chain of causation for the simple reason that every effect must have a cause, and in turn that cause must have an effect. Through this Law we can understand how vibratory control is gradually emerging from chaos into a scientifically and mathematically understood art.

7. THE LAW OF GENDER: The Law of Gender manifests in all things as masculine and feminine. It is this Law that covers what we know as creation. The Law of Gender manifests in the animal kingdom as sex. It simply proves again the Law of Polarity, the Law of Vibration, the Law of Cause and Effect, etc. Without dual principle of male and female in all things, there could not be a difference of potential nor perpetuation of motion, nor a regeneration. More than any other, this Law explains the process of mental creation, and a thorough understanding of it enables you to create any condition in life you choose, whether that condition be an increase in the "good things in life," such as more money, cars, homes, vacations, perfect health; or a greater abundance of Life's true riches, such as greater happiness, faith, spirituality and love.

An understanding of these seven Laws, together with the sub-laws that operate under them, will place you in possession of a knowledge that, when applied to the restoration of human health, will work what the world calls "WONDERS."

On the personal plane, we have the Laws of the Body, Mind, and Soul. An entire book has been written on the subject by Dr. Fleet, namely his *"RAYS OF THE DAWN,"* which is received free of charge by each new enrollee of the Institute. The Institute has summarized these laws into two charts, upon which they are depicted as follows:

If You Are
Off The Beam
You Will Have Disease

1. INCORRECTLY COMBINED MEALS

2. IMPROPER MUSCULAR EXERCISE

3. IMPROPER RECUPERATION

4. IMPROPER EXTERNAL AND INTERNAL SANITATION

5. FEAR

6. WORRY

7. SELFISHNESS

8. VANITY

9. ANGER

10. CRITICISM

11. ENVY

12. GREED

13. HYPOCRISY

14. PREJUDICE

15. JEALOUSY

16. HATE

The above named Laws are the so-called negative Laws, and apply mostly to the mind. They apply to all of us, but so do the positive Laws, or the Laws of the soul, which are depicted on the chart as follows:

If You Are
On The Beam
You Will Have Health

1. CORRECTLY BALANCED MEALS

2. PROPER MUSCULAR EXERCISE

3. PROPER RECUPERATION

4. EXTERNAL AND INTERNAL SANITA-TION

5. FAITH

6. HOPE

7. GENEROSITY-CHARITY

8. ASPIRATION

9. PATIENCE

10. SYMPATHY

11. NON-INTERFERENCE

12. KINDNESS

13. COURAGE

14. FORGIVENESS

15. DUTY

16. LOVE

These latter Laws are the positive Laws of the Soul, and to the degree that they are allowed to express will place one closer and closer to the state known as universal or cosmic consciousness. For those people who can express these Laws fully, the dawning of Cosmic Day, or the Fourth Dimensional Realm of Being, will be at hand. This entails a definite process of evolution of the human soul, and before such *evolvement* is possible, we must learn how to *involve* first. The methods whereby this may be accomplished will be elaborated upon in the next chapter.

CHAPTER FIVE

"The Key to the Fourth Dimension:

KNOW THYSELF"

THE PRAYER

Please let me first and always examine myself
Let me be honest and truthful
Let me seek and assume responsibility
Let me understand rather than be understood
Let me trust and have faith in myself and my
    fellow man
Let me love rather than be loved
Let me give rather than receive.

(Synanon Prayer)

In this chapter we will discuss the various methods whereby we may come to know ourselves, and references will be given to various institutions which are helpful in regards to this endeavor. In getting to know ourselves, we effectively lift the lid of the pit of ignorance, and will find to our amazement that there was really nothing down there to be scared of after all. "On the contrary," says CONCEPT-THERAPY, "once the base emotions expressed are sublimated, they lose all power over us; for through proper understanding we assume control over them."

TRUE FRIEND. Have you ever noticed how you can solve everyone else's problem but not your own? This is because your emotion drives your understanding, and clouds your thinking ability. The mind is constructed to be able to think of one thing at a time only, and will normally pursue the negative tendency to focus in on the unpleasant manifestations of the problem at hand, rather than applying constructive thought towards the solution. It is for this reason that in getting your analysis underway it would be most helpful to enlist the aid of a friend in whom you can have strict confidence, and, who like yourself, desires to attain the goal of self-purification, peace of mind, and cosmic consciousness. The idea is to sit down together and talk "gut-level" feelings, namely those things we normally feel but are ashamed to talk about. For instance, you should talk about your true feelings regarding your friend's appearance, mode of dress, pleasing as well as annoying mannerisms, without being afraid that you'll insult him, and looking him or her straight in the eye while talking to him. This should be done with love where possible, coupled with the full realization that you are opening yourself to a similar good-natured attack from your friend.

Difficult to do?
You bet!
Worthwhile and rewarding?
Very definitely!

This straight-forward method of soul-surgery cannot help but produce lasting and beautiful results, providing that the common goal be kept in mind at all times, and personality-hurts are kept at a minimum by giving vent to them in adult fashion, instead of repressing them. In addition you will build the most meaningful friendship of your life. During such get-togethers it is well to keep in mind that:

—little minds discuss things
—mediocre minds discuss people, and
—great minds discuss ideas.

EYEBALLING. This technique is extremely beneficial, and can be a great deal of fun in the form of a game. It simply consists of looking each other straight in the eyes without speaking a word. This can be done for a specific period of time, at which both participants quit, or it may be persisted in until one of the participants "gives up."

Once you have gained proficiency with this technique, you will gain much self-confidence in extending its use into your daily relations with people, by making an effort to look them straight in the eyes while talking to them. While at first this may be difficult to do, you will find that with practice it becomes natural, and your higher nature will manifest its approval of your determination by rewarding you with a feeling of inner strength and ever-increasing self-confidence.

PSYCHO-ANALYSIS. According to **CONCEPT-THERAPY,** "man unknowingly represses and keeps down in the subconscious depths everything that he doesn't understand or is ashamed of, not realizing that these urges, feelings and inclinations that influence his very life are really emotional memories striving for expression. If man could be educated as to the nature and impact of these emotions and the process by which he inherited them, he would be in a position to control them."

Due to his lack of knowledge of this fact, however, he represses them to the extent that they must find expression in a different way; the force with which they evenually materialize often resulting in some sort of abnormal expression. Though the acts which he performs may be "normal" from the individual point of view, they may be judged to be "abnormal" as seen through the social censor of conventional opinion. Unless man can handle the conflicts that arise from this perpetual double standard, he will become abnormal in some way, and "develop peculiar ideas, mannerisms, and odd, illogical viewpoints of life. These habits of thought and action are called complexes, which prevent the individual from living the life of a normal, healthy human being. Thus he confuses his mind and warps his soul, and in the end becomes permanently bewildered and confused himself." (Concept-Therapy).

Man possesses two distinct and separate forms of consciousness; viz. His own human consciousness (known as his conscious mind) which he has acquired, and the spiritual consciousness (known as the sub-conscious mind) which he has inherited. Quoting Concept-Therapy further, "It is the clash between these two forms of consciousness that is responsible for the majority of man's physical, mental, and spiritual ills. Pre-historic man was not subject to many of the diseases which afflict modern man, because prehistoric man generally gave expression to the thoughts and the emotions that he experienced. Modern man, on the other hand, rather than expressing or sublimating his thoughts and emotions, often represses them, causing physical and mental abnormalities."

The subconscious is forever trying to make man conscious of the causes of his problems by communicating these causes to him in the form of dreams. This is where psycho-analysis is immensely helpful, because as one of its tools it utilizes and interprets your dreams as a medium to diagnose the cause of your problems. If, like most people, you are not adept when it comes to proper dream analysis, and you feel that inner conflicts and tensions have reached such a point that you need help with them, you will do well to place yourself under the care of a competent psychoanalyst. You should do so with the full intention of eventually terminating such help, however, realizing at the outset that his help will only be a stepping stone for you—a learning procedure—as it were, until you become strong enough to "make it" on your own.

This attitude is extremely important. Do not misinterpret it to mean that you should be on the defensive, however, because nothing could be farther from the truth. Complete honesty where possible is by far the best policy towards a rapid cure. Your analyst can only help you as much as you let him, and it is well to realize that in the final analysis you must help yourself, since all analysis is really self-analysis. All the analyst can do is to direct your mind towards the cure; ultimately all psychoanalysis must be conducted in the mind of the patient and not in the mind of the analyst.

GROUP THERAPY. While psycho-analysis is one of the best methods available, it has the double disadvantage of being both time consuming and expensive. Therefore, if you cannot afford individual psychoanalysis, group therapy may be the answer. Many such groups exist, either under the auspices of organizations dedicated to that purpose or under the direction of local psychologists, family counselors, psychiatrists or psycho-therapists. Rather than there being a one-to-one patient-doctor relationship, the group as a whole acts as a censor; thus the additional benefit is gained by being evaluated by more than one person. Assuming you are not too much on the defensive, this provides you with an excellent opportunity to come to see yourself as others see you. Eventually group therapy will awaken within you the ability to make your own decisions, endowing you with the equipment necessary to resist unfair attacks upon your personality, yet an open enough mind to properly evaluate and reason upon fair observations pertaining to your character. Thus priceless self-confidence is gained.

SYNANON GAME. The Synanon game is a very unique form of group therapy. For one thing, there's no leader. There's just people who are sincerely trying to better themselves. Briefly, about ten to fifteen people get together in a room for some two-three hours, during which time they endeavor to talk true "gut-level" feelings rather than allowing each other to get by with the petty rationalizations that so often are allowed to slip away "unnoticed" in regular forms of group therapy. As such, I feel that it is only fair to warn you that in order to play the Synanon game, a strong constitution is needed — a tough skin, so to speak—coupled with an earnest desire to become a better and a more relaxed human being. According to the founder of Synanon, Charles Diederich:— "The Synanon game has roots as old as man. I am convinced that Jesus and his disciples played an early form of the game. There were thirteen of them, which would be just about the right number. I am further convinced that the phrase in the Bible: 'confess ye to one another' is additional evidence of an ancient group situation that was held without a priest or witch doctor or primitive psychiatrist." Says Guy Endore "The Synanon game deals very effectively with the mess of memories and emotions, the broth of philosophy and religion, the tangle of wisdom and ignorance, the confusion of what is right and what is wrong—all of which is cooking inside a human being, and which cries out to express itself." "Human beings tend to become too deeply attached to the self-image they have contrived for themselves. While this self-image is needed by everyone, people are generally far too sensitive and protective about it, guarding it as if it were their very life."

"It is just this image," continues Guy Endore in his

pamphlet *The Human Sport;* "that the sportsmen of the game try to smash, and that every other person rushes to defend. And it is out of this combat, practiced again and again, that the player gradually builds for himself not necessarily a different self-image, but one more flexible, one that can take plenty of blows without going to pieces."

Says Mr. Endore: "The Synanon game makes you grow up, and not just swell your muscles. You will discover, often to your own surprise, that you have changed without knowing it. Often the cure of your problem was merely an incident within the educational process that lay concealed in the game." By and by you will come to understand the true significance of the Synanon Philosophy, adapted from Emerson's remarks as follows:

THE SYNANON PHILOSOPHY

"The Synanon Philosophy is based on the belief that there comes a time in everyone's life when he arrives at the conviction that envy is ignorance; that imitation is suicide; that he must accept himself for better or for worse as is his portion; that though the wide universe is full of good, no kernel of nourishing corn can come to him but through his toil bestowed on that plot of ground which is given to him to till. The power which resides in him is new in nature, and none but he knows what it is that he can do, nor does he know until he has tried. Bravely let him speak the utmost syllable of his conviction. God will not have his work made manifest by cowards.

A man is relieved and gay when he has put his heart

into his work and done his best; but what he has said or done otherwise shall give him no peace. As long as he willingly accepts himself, he will continue to grow and develop his potentialities. As long as he does not accept himself, much of his energies will be used to defend rather than to explore and actualize himself.

No one can force a person towards permanent and creative learning. He will learn only if he wills to. Any other type of learning is temporary and inconsistent with the self and will disappear as soon as the threat is removed. Learning is possible in an environment that provides information, the setting, materials, resources, and by his being there. God helps those who help themselves."

WRITING ANALYSIS. Possessing the required fundamental knowledge as to the workings of the human personality, writing analysis is an excellent road towards more complete self-knowledge. The rules are simple: Set aside an hour each day during which time you sit down with pen in hand and write down immediately every thought that comes into your mind. As at times thoughts come very rapidly, it is well that you learn to abbreviate certain key phrases. As before, the idea is to be ruthlessly honest with yourself. As you read your writings, you will begin to detect certain patterns and thinking habits towards which your mind seems to return time and time again. Remaining as objective as possible, you will begin to see yourself in a different light and gain incentive to change those habits of thought which keep you in a negative mental rut, while amplifying or leaving undisturbed the constructive patterns that are there. To

get the greatest possible benefit out of your writing analysis, you should place no resrictions whatsoever upon the
thoughts, feelings and type of language that comes to mind
to describe these thoughts and feelings. Since the writing
is done in private, there should be no objection to putting
down precisely what is in your thoughts. To convey the
idea as to what a typical writing analysis looks like, I will
include a few excerpts of a typical analysis; in which the
incidents are real, but the names have been changed:

5-28—: Foremost thing on my mind continues to be
Ann. I am confused about trying to forget her, because in
a way she's self-torture to me, yet I should love her as a
fellow human being. Her note seemed cold this morning,
yet I keep wondering. I suppose loneliness is a big part of
it, if I had some steady girl-friend it'd be easier. But
can't see going steady with any of the girls I've been dating
lately. Weird, but it seems that everybody's "great love"
is always just around the corner, but never there at this
moment in time! Don't even want to look at the implications right now—some other time. Had very childish
emotions about Ann; I was going to the party with Lynn,
hoping Ann would show up and see me with Lynn and get
jealous. While part of me wants to let her go, another
part wants to keep hanging on, creating one H . . . of
a lot pressure and conflict. I sure play some pretty
s . . . . games. I am wondering what will become of the
kids—no sense for me to worry about it, I guess. They are
not my kids anyway. I'd probably felt different if I'd been
their real dad. Hear clock ticking and traffic outside. It's
raining. Legs are shaking. Wonder how many emotions I've
repressed. I am very impatient as I am doing this; won-

der if I should listen to tapes instead and how much time I should spend at it. Hear refrigerator. Wonder about Julie—don't feel much for her—her superficiality bothers me I suppose.

6-3—Started off really disgusted today. G . . . . ! Went to probation department, found out I'll probably be strapped with bill for kids as long as they are in juvenile hall. I just don't understand this whole d . . . . mess. Want to stop smoking, but too nervous right now. I am scared of marriage right now, why do I have such a hang-up about women that have had much sex before or that date a lot? Some bind! I am only interested in pretty women yet they are the ones that date much, so I can feel bad or jealous or "good" when I bow out yet never tell them why. Pretty childish of me, fella! Why hang-up about . . . etc.? Cause momma drove it into me, I suppose, she and her g . . . . puritan ideas about sex, and her s . . . . puritan ideas about "neat" girls, vs. "bad" girls, etc. Been writing 20 min. now, vague feeling about socks and stinking feet. Airplanes in war. I saw it much longer than other people there. Seem to have war obsession, everytime I see war pictures it reminds me. Wonder if I use it as an attention-getter, though. Bombs were falling, and broke windows. I wasn't afraid. Barber was going to clip my head bald then, cause I'd challenged him to, yet didn't want him to. Remember lying in a ditch, hiding from the Germans. Sister told me I saw people get killed, but can't remember, must have suppressed. Maybe brain'll release significant memories. Should get other paper for this. Wonder about my speech and inner nature. Why can't I ever be satisfied with what

I have? Why must I always select something to worry about? Hope self-hypnosis will discover that. Getting better at it. Wonder just how deep I can go. Will stop for now.

8-7—Got rid of another hang-up this morning. Man did it hurt coming out. But did it feel good and FREE when it did!! FREEDOM! Funny how little things can run your life for you. From now on I am going to make an effort to run my body, instead of allowing its desires to run me and keep me uptight. I am getting much more relaxed; am beginning to see people now, and I am beginning to see my mother as a human being. Can understand her and forgive her now. I am learning how to meditate and concentrate, can solve many problems that way. I am even beginning to see God in things. I am taking my responsibilities more and more seriously lately. Today noticed wind playing with my hair and somehow felt the wind was conscious of me; the earth too! Beautiful feeling! Funny how the world changes as I change my thoughts.

From the foregoing few excerpts you can readily perceive the central idea. The first two examples were episodes that occurred shortly upon divorce; the third excerpt was written almost a year afterwards, at which time many adjustments were made, but many as yet remained to be made. In this way we are able to "dig out" and neutralize many subconscious habit patterns that were previously playing havoc with our happiness, tranquillity, and peace of mind. Note that rather than attempting to begin digging into childhood memories right away, it is far better to let the mind just wander, for sooner or later it will take you there by the association of ideas.

MENTAL CATHARSIS OR SELF ANALYSIS. This method is in reality not too different from writing analysis, and my major purpose is to explain the process in a somewhat different light. While writing analysis is extremely beneficial at first; you will come to a point where you can learn to immediately evaluate and check wrong thinking patterns as they occur without having to write them down anymore. While the methods herein discussed are all very effective in bringing about the desired results, one very important missing link transcends them all, and that is their failure to replace that which was given up or lost with something new and better, such as a workable and meaningful philosophy of life. It is in this respect that the CONCEPT-THERAPY INSTITUTE is by far the most complete service that I have found upon the subject, for *in addition to offering an entire course in methods of self-analysis, it offers the most complete, the most logical and the most beautiful philosophy of life that I have ever come in contact with.* The different light in which I wish to explain the process of Mental Catharsis is the light in which it is discussed by the founder of CONCEPT-THERAPY, Dr. Thurman Fleet: "As the name mental catharsis implies, this process is of a cathartic, cleansing, purifying nature. In MENTAL CATHARSIS a determined effort is made to eliminate from the system many objectionable emotional states, resentments, grudges, old "sores" and "bruises" by bringing them into the field of consciousness by an act of the WILL and then sterilizing or neutralizing them by the power of the light of ATTENTION, REASON, and WILL." He recommends that we: "single out the offensive tendencies by calling them by name, and turn the light of consciousness upon them—the light that penetrates every hidden crevice and exposes without reservation every hateful quality. Instead of concealing them, drive them out into the light of observation, then deal them a hearty blow with the HAMMER of the WILL directed by the FORCE of REASON, then disperse the fragments. To hide, conceal, or cover them up only means to "bury them alive," to have them work mischief for you."

"Thousands who are suffering from emotional instability and nervous conditions can do much to overcome their distress by being frank with themselves in a constructive self-analysis. It is impossible, of course, for anyone to see himself in the same light as others do. His viewpoint is subjective; theirs is objective. But if one is willing to cast off the mantle of false pride, egotism, vanity, and courage he will face his true nature, and can accomplish much toward solving his problems. Even the neurotic, if he is given the proper instruction and guidance, can through self-analysis find the cause and cure of what often appears to be an utterly hopeless and futile situation. Here is where the LAWS OF LIFE, as published in the CONCEPT-THERAPY Course, are so beneficial. They constitute an ideal medium for self-analysis."

In an attempt to clarify the nature and origin of psychological disorders, Dr. Fleet gives one of the most beautiful explanations I have ever seen: "Upon the battlefield of the human SOUL two masters are ever contending for the crown of supremacy, for the kingship and dominion of the consciousness; namely, the animal nature, or the CARNAL MAN, and the divine nature, or the SPIRITUAL MAN. The Carnal Nature is that rebellious one who employs as its weapons passion, pride, avarice, vanity, self-will — the implements of darkness. The SPIR-ITUAL nature is that meek and lowly one who utilizes the weapons of gentleness, patience, purity, sacrifice, humility, love — the instruments of LIGHT. In every soul the battle is waged, and just as a soldier cannot engage at the same time in two opposing armies, so every soul is enlisted either in the ranks of the CARNAL or the SPIRITUAL. There is no half-and-half course." This contention is well supported in the Scriptures; for example, Buddha, the teacher of Truth said: "There is the CARNAL, and there is the SPIRITUAL; where the CARNAL is, the SPIR-ITUAL is not; where the SPIRITUAL is, the CARNAL is not." Jesus, the anointed teacher, declared in reference to this inward battle that: "No man can serve two masters, for either he will hate the one and love the other, or else he will hold to one and despise the other. Ye cannot serve God and Mammon."

Continuing, Dr. Fleet says that: "By silently examining his mind, heart, and conduct, one can readily determine whether he is ascending toward the SPIRITUAL or plunging deeper into the CARNAL aspect of his nature. If you harbor thoughts of suspicion, emnity, envy, lust, pride, etc., then you are chained to your carnal nature regardless of whatever religion you may profess. If, however, you fight strenuously against these evils, persistently endeavoring to overcome them, then you are aligning yourself with the SPIRITUAL although outwardly you may profess no religion. Are you self-willed, ever seeking to gain your own ends, self-indulgent, self-centered; or is your nature gentle, mild, unselfish, devoid of every form of self-indulgence, and ever-ready to sacrifice? If you are controlled by the former, then the CARNAL is your master; if the latter, the SPIRITUAL is the object of your affection."

The conclusion today seems as inescapable as it was two thousand years ago when Jesus first delivered his Sermon on the Mount, and that is that in order to gain SPIRITUALITY we must be willing to relinquish our CARNALITY. "As one succeeds in overcoming his CARNAL nature," resumes Dr. Fleet; "he will begin to interpret things in their true light and proper relations. He who is swayed by any passion, prejudice, like or dislike, adjusts everything to that particular bias and sees only his own delusions. Absolutely free from all passionate prejudice, preference, and partiality, he becomes aware of his TRUE SELF, sees others as they really are, and views all things in their proper proportions and right relationships. Having nothing to attack, nothing to defend, nothing to conceal, and no interests to guard, he is at PEACE. He has realized the profound simplicity of the SPIRITUAL CONSCIOUSNESS, for this unbiased, tranquil, blessed state of mind is the state of TRUTH. He who attains to it dwells with the angels and sits at the footstool of the Supreme. Understanding the GREAT LAW as taught in CONCEPT-THERAPY, "GOD IS," knowing the origin of sorrow, comprehending the secret of suffering, knowing the way of emancipation in TRUTH, how can such a one engage in strife and condemnation. Though he fully realizes that the blind, self-seeking world—surrounded with the clouds of its own illusions and enveloped in the darkness of error and carnal self — cannot perceive the steadfast light of truth and that it is utterly incapable of comprehending the profound simplicity of the heart that has died, or is dying, to the carnal self; yet he also knows that when the suffering ages have piled up mountains of sorrow, the crushed and over-burdened SOUL of the world will fly to its final refuge and with the completion of the ages every prodigal son will return to the fold of TRUTH."

The person who deliberately rids himself of false concepts and limiting beliefs soon begins to develop masterful self-control and true power. This is not necessarily that power which is known as "will-power," but the subtle yet powerful force of spiritual power based upon true principle. To quote Dr. Fleet: "The difference between a man of weakness and one of power lies not in the strength of the personal will — for the stubborn man is usually weak and foolish — but in that FOCUS OF CONSCIOUSNESS which represents their states of knowledge. A man commences to develop POWER when, checking his impulses and selfish inclinations, he falls back upon the higher and calmer consciousness within him and begins to steady himself upon a PRINCIPLE. The realization of unchanging PRINCIPLES in consciousness is at once the source and secret of the highest power.

When after much searching, suffering, and sacrificing, the light of an ETERNAL PRINCIPLE dawns upon the the SOUL, a divine calm ensues and joy unspeakable gladdens the heart. He who has realized such PRINCIPLE ceases to wonder, and remains poised and self-possessed. He no longer is a slave to passion but becomes a master builder in the TEMPLE OF DESTINY."

"As you proceed — through self-analysis day by day detaching yourself more and more from your carnal nature, the LOVE that is selfless will gradually become revealed to you. And when you are growing patient and calm, as your petulances, tempers and irritabilities are passing away from you, and the more powerful lusts and prejudices cease to enslave you, THEN will you know that DIVINE awakening within you, drawing you ever nearer to the ETERNAL HEART, not far from that SELFLESS LOVE, the possession of which is peace and immortality.

To grow in self-control, in patience, in equanimity is to grow in strength and power, and you can thus develop only by focussing your consciousness upon a PRINCIPLE. The principle as taught in CONCEPT-THERAPY (and well supported by the statements of Jesus the Christ) is that GOD IS WITHIN YOU, striving to express Himself through your BODY, MIND, and SOUL. Once you bring these component parts into harmony with the LAWS that govern them, then GOD and YOU have become as ONE, and like Jesus you will be able to say, "I and my Father are One." The Divine adventure for you will be accomplished, and you will have attained to PEACE and IMMORTALITY."

"Break away from the tyranny of custom, tradition, conventionality, and the opinion of others, until you succeed in walking lonely and erect among men. Rely upon your own judgment. Be true to your own conscience. Follow the LIGHT that is within you, for all outward lights are so many will-o'-the wisps. There will be those who will tell you that you are foolish, that your judgment is faulty, that your conscience is all awry, etc., but heed them not. If what they say is true, the sooner YOU as a seeker for wisdom find out the truth about yourself, the better. And you can make this discovery only by bringing your powers to the test; therefore pursue your course bravely. Your conscience is at least your own, and to follow it is to be a man; to follow the conscience of another is to be a slave. You will experience many falls, endure many buffets, and suffer many wounds for a time, but PRESS ON in FAITH, believing that certain victory lies ahead. Search for a rock, a PRINCIPLE, and having found it, cling to it, get it under your feet and stand erect upon it, until at last immovably fixed upon it, you succeed in defying the fury of the waves and storms of selfishness.

Selfishness in any and every form is dissipation, weakness, death. Unselfishness in its spiritual aspect is conservation, power, life. As you grow in spiritual life and become established upon principles, you will become as beautiful and as unchangeable as those principles, will taste of their immortal essence, and will realize the eternal and indestructible nature of the GOD within. Self-analysis, honestly made, is a wonderful way of seeing yourself as you really are, but of what value or use is self-analysis if the person is insincere? To get a true picture of your innermost self and then do nothing to remedy your faults is an excellent way to hate yourself for what you are. On the other hand, if one has the correct philosophy of life, if he believes what Jesus said that the Kingdom of Heaven is HERE, NOW, and can be entered provided one is worthy, then self-analysis is the KEY with which you may unlock the door."

In conclusion, Dr. Fleet states that: "Very little illness has its root in physical causes. Most of it comes from the violation of NATURAL LAW which governs the BODY, MIND, and SOUL, and it is almost futile to attempt to treat people unless they are, at the same time, TAUGHT HOW TO LIVE WITH THEMSELVES. That is the grand purpose of CONCEPT-THERAPY."

The tremendous value of self-analysis has long been recognized by the world's great thinkers: for instance, Thomas Jefferson, one of the greatest men that America has ever produced, once said: "Fix firmly reason in her seat and call to her tribunal every fact and every opinion. Question with boldness even the existence of a God, because if there be one He must approve of the homage of reason rather than that of blindfold fear. Your own reason is the only oracle given you by heaven, and you are answerable not for the righteousness but for the uprighteousness of the decision." Herbert Spencer, another man of considerable stature, has aptly stated: "When a man's knowledge is not in order, the more of it he has the greater will be his confusion." Another great thinker has said: "We praise the man who has the courage of his convictions, but every bigot and fanatic has that. What is much harder and rarer, is to have the courage to re-examine one's convictions and to reject them if they don't square with the facts."

If such are the opinions of some of the world's greatest thinkers, it stands to reason that self-analysis is immensely valuable in one's emotional growth. Unless we are clean of heart and pure of mind we cannot attain to any degree of spiritual consciousness, and continue to grow in AWARENESS until the supreme state of spiritual consciousness, namely COSMIC CONSCIOUSNESS, is reached. Indeed, SELF-ANALYSIS, honestly made, is THE KEY TO THE FOURTH DIMENSION.

CHAPTER SIX

The Storm

THE AGONY AND THE ECSTASY

As Confusion grips my soul in
its iron hand, thick layers
of fog obscure what I thought
was my understanding.

"Why, oh why, God . . .?" cries my anguished
soul. "Why am I, and why doth Thou
thus test me? What is the meaning
of it all?"

I want to know the answers so much
that I am willing to give up everything
I have for them.
But none come . . .

Suddenly, the still small voice
speaks to me and bids me to endure
a little while longer.
"Only the patient may partake of the
most glorious of visions," it reminds me
once again.
And once again I resign in glorious anticipation.

You have an enemy. Yourself. The False you we know as "ego," which has kept all of us in ignorance and bondage all these years, while our Real Self rebelled. And rebelled. For our Real Self is our Soul, and It does not like the narrow confines we have limited It to by erroneous thinking. Because It must be FREE and *absolutely limitless* to satisfy its True Nature. That's why we feel so "low" at times without apparent reason. That's why our boat may be rocked so easily at times. For at those times we have knowingly inhibited the expression of our true nature and this is the only way our soul can tell us that we have performed wrong action. For if we could be happy all of the time, we'd never see our mistakes, such as the games we all are apt to play at times, those socially accepted games that nevertheless go against our true nature. It is our true nature to be free and creative, and if we will analyze it closely, we will find that this is exactly what we always dream and daydream about. Since we've consciously repressed the voice of our soul from reaching us most of the time, we've left it no choice but to communicate with us when our thinking faculty is inactive. Such as in dreams. Or when we're very quiet and allow our mind to travel amidst the lofty visions we create, which visions represent the way we feel things ought to be. Our soul is always ready to communicate with us; whenever we want it to. It does so in the form of that "still, small voice," the voice of conscience.

When you think about it, that's really the only judge we have. That ever-present, nagging feeling coming from somewhere inside us, telling us that we may think that we get by with things, but we never get past our own internal judge. Or around it. It doesn't care about what *we* feel is

right or wrong either; and that which may be right to us
may be wrong to it, and vice versa. Interpreting actions as
right or wrong against the rigid and inflexible criterion
of Universal Consciousness, it is not concerned with our
personal wishes or vague interpretations of 'good' and
'bad', or 'oughts' and 'ought nots'. We have all tried to
please other people at times, by giving in to their expectations of us, such expectations having risen in the wake of
nebulous social values as to what is the "right" or "wrong"
thing to do. And whenever we gave in, we felt badly about
it afterwards, as though we'd "sold out." We found that
other people weren't really pleased when we gave in, and
that they began to demand more and more of us, being
less and less pleased — and more "expecting" — in return.
Of course, if we went to the other extreme by only thinking of ourselves and overlooking other people's feelings,
we soon found that we wound up just as miserable.

What, then, is the right approach?

Simple.

We must learn to listen to our conscience. How? Many
ways. For a start, we can get ourselves a hand-mirror, lie
down in some quiet place and look at ourselves, the best
time being just upon arising or before retiring. We should
be sure that all ideas of vanity have disappeared from our
thinking, for holding such thoughts can only impede our
progress. In fact, we should try and still our mind completely. We should imagine a large cave in the rocks with
absolutely nothing in it, and liken it unto our mind, as we
are looking at ourselves. However we do it, we must be
sure that our attitude is completely receptive towards
whatever realizations may come. And come they will.
One by one, slowly but surely. At first the signals will

be vague and uncertain. The reason for this can be explained by the following analogy: Imagine a bright light bulb shining forth radiantly. You then proceed to cover it with thin, transparent layers of paper. Having completed the first layer, you put on a second layer, a third one, and so on, using increasingly denser and thicker paper as you build layers. Finally the light which shines through can hardly be perceived, although it's unmistakably there. You are now reversing the process. Through self-analysis you are removing the first thick layers of paper in the form of erroneous ideas, false concepts, "hang-ups," etc., causing them to fall away from you. As you progress, the soul light of conscience is able to shine forth more brightly than before, and its voice becomes more and more distinguishable from the voice of the false ego self.

The false self will put up a battle, and you must be prepared to fight it. It is helpful to remember at all times that the soul forever seeks to break the shell of ignorance which imprisons it, and though some pain may be endured during the breaking of the shell, it is inevitable that the shell be broken. Just like it is inevitable for the ready to be born chick to break the shell which encloses it. Actually the pain is nothing but illusion anyway, for it is only the false ego self that gives rise to it; it employs pain as a weapon to keep you from dethroning it. You must remember, however, that the soul will constantly seek freedom, and will forever liberate itself; the process of its liberation being as inevitable as the unfoldment of a flower, or the emergence of a beautiful butterfly from a caterpillar. We really don't have much choice in the matter, and the sooner we make our decision, the sooner will we gain our precious freedom. But we must pay a price for it, the price being the subjugation of our carnal self to our spiritual self. Therefore, if you should decide for freedom of the soul, you must resolve to get on with the job. Rejoice, knowing that at last the shell of ignorance is being broken. You will begin to seek the proper knowledge with which to nourish your unfolding soul, such knowledge being to the Soul what food is to the body. It is then that you will find the philosophy of CONCEPT-THERAPY to be extremely beneficial, for it gives you all the knowledge you need.

Another method you may use involves the use of any small object. The best objects are small pieces of jewelry, especially those that seem to have depth to them.

Place the object upon a simple, completely uncluttered background. This may be an empty table, a large piece of felt, or a plain piece of paper. You may fasten it to the paper so that it can be held in an upright position.

Having made these preparations, you are now ready to go to work. Get in as comfortable a sitting position as you can and proceed to concentrate upon the object, pinpointing your attention upon it in such a way that you allow no other thoughts to enter your mind. Constantly push distracting thoughts out of your mind as you continue to concentrate. Though at first this is very difficult, and you cannot stop these thoughts from coming, you can at least send them on their way. Endeavor to make your mind an absolute blank, and listen quietly and receptively to the voice of the Spirit (conscience) within. The more you practice this technique, the more meaningful it will become. You are creating in your mind a safe and tranquil haven towards which you will be able to retreat time and time again when the pressures of outside living threaten to get you down. Once you have developed this treasure, you will reap untold blessings through its use.

A third method for calming the raging tides of your mind and thus developing the proper method by which you may communicate with the Spirit within involves the use of self-hypnosis. While in the hypnotic state, you are more aware, sensitive, and suggestible than you are in the normal state, and it is during this time that you will want to impress your subconscious mind with whatever suggestion you wish to "take hold." Bearing in mind that the sub-conscious carries out negative suggestions just as effectively as positive ones, you may wish to gather additional information about how to place suggestions properly, etc. Much information is available, especially from the Concept-Therapy Institute.

The use of a tape recorder is recommended to produce the relaxed state. You may tape the recording yourself, and it will be a good idea for you to leave a five-minute blank on the tape after you have reached the hypnotic state, during which time you allow impressions to come in. Right after this five minute blank, place the suggestion that, upon re-entering the conscious state you will remember in detail the impressions that your subconscious has given you. If you feel that you are not familiar enough with the subject of hypnosis to apply any of the techniques yourself, you will find many books and records available that will teach you the techniques involved. In addition, many short term classes are also available upon the subject; just scan the ads in your local newspaper. According to Ed Harmon, of Tustin, California, self-hypnosis is becoming an increasingly popular method of relaxation with many people.

Hypnosis is particularly valuable in that you will come to realize that it is really de-hypnosis. Through its consistent use the time will come that you will comprehend that that which you now consider the real world is in reality the false, illusionary one, and vice versa.

The fourth method we will discuss is that of meditation, which is really nothing more nor less than a method of abstract thinking, or deep thought. Several records and many books are available on this subject also. The two records I have found quite valuable are those made by Roy Masters of the Foundation for Human Understanding in Los Angeles, in which the entire process and purpose is explained in detail. Should you wish to practice meditation, you may purchase these records from the Foundation.

This process involves the quieting of your mind, and is best practiced in the early morning just upon arising, or in the evening just before retiring. The idea is to concentrate your mind upon some object or subject, such as a part of your body. Anything will do really, as long as you are able to concentrate on it and thus can keep your mind off your problems for a while. Become acutely aware of your object of concentration — thus allowing your mind to work upon itself. As it does, your problems will vanish almost imperceptibly, and answers will come more and more rapidly as you continue. Instead of wasting your efforts upon attempted solutions to your problems put the same amount of concentration into your exercise of meditation, and you will be amazed at how your problems seem to take care of themselves. The beginning of Wisdom is the realization that the thing you are anxious about today won't seem important tomorrow.

The fifth, and by far the best method, is that of imaging, used by the Concept-Therapy Institute. All you need to do is to form a vivid mental picture of whatever you desire, and hold on to that picture no matter what happens. Sooner or later that picture will manifest. It makes no difference whether the picture represents a material object or a state of mind (happiness, for instance).

Whenever new ideas are brought into existence, or old ones are re-activated, the proponent of said ideas must be prepared to deal with a certain amount of skepticism. While the ideas and techniques discussed herein are not wholly original with me, I do enthusiastically propose them for your consideration.

Having personally tried them, I KNOW that they work, but this does not necessarily convince you, the reader. To gain a conviction for yourself, you must decide to try out and apply these methods until results become apparent. The greater your determination, the sooner results will appear. It stands to reason that spending one to two hours a day towards the development of your mental and spiritual faculties is not too much when you consider that you spend some ten to twelve hours daily caring for your bodily needs.

It is a well-known fact among mystics that a skeptic is seldom willing to acquire the faculties with which he can test the hypothesis of those who have risen above skepticism. You will undoubtedly agree with me that it is only fair that you try these methods before passing final judgment. If such is your resolution, be prepared to give up your skeptic status, for in all probability you will change your mind. Keeping the goal in mind at all times — namely happiness and peace of mind — it is well to recall the statement Jesus made in this respect: "Become therefore as little children." If up to now you have not gained lasting happiness and peace of mind your way, you will agree that it makes sense that you should try another, and to become as a little child, meaning to have the FAITH and the TRUST a little child does in the application of these methods. Seeing what these simple tests can do for you, you will then "get the full impact" of what CONCEPT-THERAPY can do for you, if you give it a chance!

FREE WILL VS. PREDESTINATION. We will now take up and attempt to discuss the subject upon which religions have battled since time immemorial; namely that of free will vs. predestination. Presumably you have thought about this question at various times during your life. "If we are predestined," you may say, "why should I bother to go through the trouble of analyzing myself; study anything; or learn how to concentrate my mind? It's all 'in the bag' anyway, and there's nothing I can do about it." I would like to answer your question with another one, if I may: Could it be that you are predestined to read this book and either to apply or reject its proposed methods? If you are 100% for predestination, the conclusion is inescapable, and I ask you to ponder it well.

"If we have free will," others may say, "then it is up to me, and me alone to either reject or apply these methods. It is I* who of my own free will chose to read this book, the circumstances leading up to my perusal being guided simply by chance. It is I who decides whether the author's suggestions are worthy of consideration or not, and upon that basis I decide whether I will give the proposed

*Referring to the *personal* I, rather than the *impersonal* one.

methods a try—or vice versa. I am for Free Will 100%, and it is I who make all the decisions in my life."

Are you really? If that were true you should be able to decide not to feel bad for no reason at all, and not to react negatively to an unpleasant stimulus or situation. Ask yourself these questions also: "When getting up from a chair do *I* decide which muscle groups to flex and which to relax to accomplish the act? Do I decide which thoughts enter my mind, and which thoughts don't? Did I decide where I would be born, at what time of the year, and did I determine to what race, color, creed, or sex I'd belong? Again, dear reader, I ask you to ponder this very deeply.

Most people have not taken a definite stand on the Free-Will vs. Predestination question, but are hanging somewhere in between. Having decided that it cannot be resolved one way or the other, they feel that further thought upon the matter would be wasteful of time and energy.

Not true!

The answer is really very simple, as is the explanation to many apparent paradoxes in nature. It requires thought, however, and the type of thinking necessary can best be illustrated by the following examples: Imagine yourself to be the parent of a child to whom you've given a choice between a dish of spinach and a dish of ice-cream. From the child's point of view, the act to follow is free will, for he has free choice between the spinach and the ice-cream. At the same time, however, you *know* the child and his *inclinations,* and based upon this knowledge of him you realize that he will choose one over the other—presumably the ice-cream over the spinach—and as such his act was predestined. In other words, the act was one of free-will and one of predestination at one and the same time, the two concepts being perfectly harmonious and reconcilable. Another example is that of a mouse which has been placed into a maze by the psychological experimenter. The experimenter knows that ultimately the mouse will make it, and as such the whole thing is predestined to turn out all-right, no matter how many wrong choices the mouse might make in its exercise of free will. Yet one more example, since this is such an important question: Suppose you gave a dog a choice between a pile of silver dollars and a pile of hamburgers. While the dog, from its point of view, had free choice in the matter, it will invariably choose the pile of hamburgers, and as such its act was predestined.

Extending this line of reasoning a bit further, we can readily perceive that we stand in the same relation to our Creator as our children stand to us. While we have free choice in the questions that are placed before us, the Creator knows what our inclinations are and therefore knows which way we will choose. Studying the foregoing implications deeply, the entire question becomes perfectly natural, un-perplexing, and acceptable. We will realize that while our false self needs the security of being able to choose freely, our true self needs no such false security, and is perfectly happy to play its pre-destined role, because its will is the will of the One, for the true self *is* the One.

Thus it can be seen that we are neither totally free agents devoid of all responsibility, nor are we the helpless pawns in the chess-game played by an inexorable Fate. For, says Dr. Fleet in his lesson on LIBERTY: "To give us hope and regard ourselves as the sport of an inexorable Fate is not LIBERTY. It is not obedience to a higher Power, but abject submission to a lower Power of IGNORANCE, UNINTELLIGENCE, and NEGATION. Perfect Liberty is the consciousness that we are not thus bound by any Power of Evil but that, on the contrary, we are centers in which the Creative Spirit of the Universe finds particular expression. Then we are in harmony with Its continual progressive movement towards still more perfect modes of expression. Therefore, Its thought and our thought, Its action and our action —become identical so that in expressing the Spirit we express Ourselves."

Somewhere along the evolutionary line, we must learn to accept the fact that to God—which is in reality our True Self or Spiritual Nature—everything just is. It is our false self that rebels against such a seemingly complex yet simple realization. The following example, borrowed from Dr. Fleet's *"Basic Principles,"* will serve to illustrate the severe limitations thinking from an ego-centered base places upon us: Imagine that you are in a Court of Law (In which supposedly the Truth reigns above all). A demonstration is about to be given, and the key actors are three men and an apple. The men are to take a bite out of the apple for the purpose of determining and testifying to its taste, but before doing so, Mr. A is to take a bite of lemon, Mr. C. will eat a little honey, while Mr. B does neither. Having completed these preliminaries, the judge now asks Mr. A to testify under oath to the taste of the apple, and Mr. A swears that it is sweet to him. Mr. C states for a fact that to him the apple is sour, while Mr. B states that to him it is neither sweet nor sour. Now, according to the Court's limited point of view, only one of these statements can be true; the question is, which one?

In adopting any one of these as truth to the exclusion of the other two the course of justice is thwarted by the court which owes its very existence to the upholding of true justice! As before, human beings fight over the apparent irreconcilability of a situation which to God just *is*. From an *ego* point of view the judge can only adopt one verdict, and in choosing one he automatically rejects two/thirds of the truth of the matter. It is this way with many of our adopted viewpoints. Normally we see only one side of a question, and while we may think we're openminded, we fail to grasp that we see only one/third of the entire matter. The portion we see is determined largely by the *beliefs* we have come to adopt over a lifetime. Should all human beings suddenly see all three aspects to any one question, strife would immediately cease, and the symbolism of the triangle, the star of David, and the pyramid would no longer be a mystery.

Are you open minded enough to check your beliefs against FACTS? Are you willing to replace erroneous beliefs with tried and true facts, even though you may find that many of the beliefs you've held dear for so long turn out to be fantasy, rather than fact, *and vice versa?* It will help you considerably to classify all of your knowledge into one of three categories, namely:

GROUP 1. FANTASY

GROUP 2. THEORY

GROUP 3. FACT

If you are in earnest, you'll take each one of your beliefs and classify it honestly and sincerely into one of the above categories, and as you do be prepared to FIGHT.

Fight what? you ask. Your false ego-self, in the form of old thought habits that feel they have a right to remain in your consciousness. The one that's responsible for all the preconceived ideas you don't think you have. Yes, it will put up a fight, as will the collective egos of your family and friends. For once you embark upon your quest for Truth, they will begin to feel that in a certain sense you are no longer one of them, and will do everything they can to "bring you to your senses." Their senses, that is. But now you know that you must find the Truth for yourself. You will have started on the Path of Attainment, and before long you'll feel as follows: "I stretch out my scrawny members and cast my eyes above. I launch myself staunchly and with confidence toward that lofty plane. It matters not that I flutter back to earth, or that I hear derisive laughter in my ears; I have started. And as I aspire to the flight of eagles, who soar with majestic serenity, someday it will come to pass. The growing knowledge will feather those members, and sureness will guide the beat of my wings. Then as I climb to the glorious heights of enlightenment, may I carry with me the knowledge that others who are still earth-bound also seek to fly. May I have the humility to refrain from losing myself in that glorious consciousness, but stay in tune with other seekers and help them find their wings." (Jim White) You will have begun the surrender of the limited to the limitless, of the finite to the Infinite, and of restriction and bondage to Freedom.

Unless you can find someone to pursue the Path to Freedom and Truth with you, you must tread upon it alone. Yet not alone. For within you is the greatest help you'll ever find. Your True Self, your Divine Counterpart.

Also upon that Path are many fellow seekers, and as you progress you will learn to recognize and get acquainted with them, while LIFE is opening up new VISTAS of glorious beauty along the way. Somewhere along the way you'll come to the full realization that you must crucify your false ego-self, and in so doing you'll grasp the full meaning of the CRUCIFIXION of Christ, which stands for the balancing of the opposites, the mastering and subjection to the WILL of the destructive emotions. Depending upon how much of a battle you allow your false self to put up you will have to endure the intensity of the STORM. It will, to put it mildly, object very strenuously against each dawning realization. Temporarily, you may lose all interest in your work, and you may, for a time, rebel against everything under the sun. All will seem topsy-turvy for a while, and you will regard everything with a suspicious eye. How long a while? Depends upon the size of your false self! The bigger the ego, the bigger the storm, and vice versa. Eventually, things will calm down. Like they've never calmed down before. You will enter a PEACE that is blissful beyond description, and everything will fall into place. Piece by piece. Life will begin to make sense; lots of it. Work will be exhilarating. The purpose of Life and your place in it will be revealed, and you will feel secure.

You will be at the helm of the Ship of Fate, for you've allowed your Real Self, your Divine Counterpart, to take over. You can now say:

"I scattered seed on a barren plain
And I watered the furrows with tears;
My heart was heavy with grief and pain
And my soul distraught with fears.
But after many weary days
Of lowering clouds and rain,
I gathered from seed that was sown in tears
A harvest of golden grain."

(Thomas Hardy)

You can now see your false self for what it truly was, and you realize how it has held you in bondage; and now you rejoice in the glorious realization that it has lost its hold over you. Forever. You now know that in reality you never had a false self to lose; only the illusion that gave rise to it. It has served its purpose, and you know what that purpose was. You will have learned the fascinating fact that the law which exists at the very center of your being is creative, and that you use the same creativeness which brought the planets into being, and which produces everything that is. The Law of your Life is really a Law of Freedom, but you have used it as a Law of Bondage. You must now use it as a Law of Freedom. You know and feel that nothing can stop you now. Knowing what you know now, how could anything stop you? For nothing can stop a Creator.

Ernest Holmes—Founder of Religious Science, sums it up this way: "We must learn to counsel with this silent partner (True Self) of ours and to accept His guidance. When we realize that our Partner makes things out of Himself by Himself becoming the things that He makes, then we shall know that no matter what undesirable facts may be in our present experience, He can dissolve them for us. Thus we transfer our burdens to this Silent Partner who has no burdens and who has no problems." You will now be able to turn around and help your fellow pathseekers, and admonish them to: "HAIL THE STORM, FOR IT IS THINE ADVERSARY COME TO STRENGTHEN THEE." For you will have learned to travel downstream in the river of consciousness, instead of battling your way against its tide by travelling upstream like you did before. As you travel downstream the river of consciousness continues to expand until it reaches the vast ocean of Oneness — the Source from whence it came.

Is it worth it? Absolutely! But it takes determination. Lots of it.

You will be happy to know that help is available if you want it. Help that will show you how to place your careful first steps on the road to Freedom, and that is there as you progress. Help that will guide you all along the way, from your first uncertain, faltering steps to your last certain, determined strides. Help that is logical, warm and humane. Help that will point out the pitfalls of the path to you. Help that will provide Friends with a capital "F". The kinds of Friends you probably thought did not exist. Friends that will bring you a realization of the meaning of True Friendship, and of Divine Indifference.

Where can you find such help? All over this country, and that's the most fortunate part of it, for the CONCEPT-THERAPY INSTITUTE has members and teachers in nearly every major city of the United States. If you drop them a card requesting information about the Institute, its program, and the address of your local teacher they will be happy to oblige. More than happy. For they are real people, interested in helping you with your problems; which they feel are also their problems.

LIFE'S MISSION

A fine peacock said to a worm one day
"Go, crawl on your lawn, and keep away
From your betters, you are ugly and slow.
Of what use are you anyway? Go away, Go!"

The worm turned a disdainful eye on the bird
And crawled a bit nearer, to make sure he was heard,
"Oh thing of glitter and outward display,
Of what use are you now, do tell me, pray?

When you spread your wide tail so haughtily,
And strut around looking so foolishly,
A warning you are for all men to see,
Against pride and arrogance and vanity.

Now watch me carefully." And as he spoke
A wondrous thing happened—his furry old cloak
Fell apart, and out from the shell—a vision
Of beauty fluttered from its prison.

A butterfly gay looked down on the bird,
And again the worm's voice—though changed, was heard.
"The worm is, you see, a part of God's plan,
And brings a deep message from Him to man.

Nothing so low, but within it is hidden
Divine radiance, which unfolds when 'tis bidden.
Man's mission here in this Life—to uncover
This beauty buried deep in himself and another."

From: Whispering Truth.

CHAPTER SEVEN

"Tributes to Concept-Therapy"

TRANQUILITY

The message of peace within the song of the birds is carried gently upon the velvet wings of the wind. All the Earth, if you but listen, conveys the same grand message of Unity and Peace. How you depend upon her! And she upon you! For as you breathe, you exhale that which becomes food for the plants, which in turn provide you with the Life principle and substance you need.

All is system, all is balance, all is rhythmic breathing in and breathing out, half the world doing one, and half the other, each depending upon the other.

In this vast ocean of intelligence, all is beauty, yea, all is peace.

One of the most eminently qualified teachers the Institute has is Reverend Crump—affectionately referred to as "Rev" by his many friends.

For one thing, he graduated from college with a degree in electrical engineering. This career, however, failed to provide many of the answers that his active and inquisitive mind was seeking, and feeling that the scientific field of engineering apparently couldn't answer his many questions, 'Rev' ultimately abandoned electrical engineering and returned to school; this time to earn a degree in Theology. Upon completing his schooling for the ministry 'Rev' served for a number of years as a highly respected and deeply loved Methodist Minister.

Possessing a double background of both science and religion, his mind was still a long way from being at rest, but kept yearning after the answers both of them had failed to provide; whatever such answers might turn out to be. As time went on, he'd gotten "glimpses" of the answer in both of his careers, but rather than settle him down, such glimpses only provided him with the determination to intensify his quest.

Electricity, he found, was really a great unknown and tremendous power, and man is very ignorant as to how this power works. To the degree that man understands its laws, however, he can make electricity do his bidding. Whether the final outcome of such utilization is positive or negative; i.e. whether it is being used to light a house or to electrocute a man, makes absolutely no difference to the power of electricity itself; it simply works for those who use it, being indifferent to the consequences of such use.

Then there was this strange Unknown Power in his work in the church, which Power had been responsible for his achievement of several "miraculous" cures during his career as a minister. Several times, through prayer and *suggestion,* he had been able to cure people who had been given up for dead by their physicians. What was it, he wondered, in what he said, did, or suggested, that "turned loose" the healing factor and thus brought about a cure in cases where all else had failed? What was this great Unknown Power, so reminiscent of the great unknown power of electricity? How was it possible for him to make a man walk who for 10 years had suffered from paralysis, and who had been given up for lost by institutions such as John Hopkins and the Mayo clinic?

After the cure, the man had shown up in church for the first time in over ten years, and gave a moving testimony about the "miracle" of the healing. "Of course it wasn't a miracle at all," Rev. said: "once you understand the Laws as taught in CONCEPT-THERAPY. I simply gave the man a new CONCEPT, a new Idea, and as such the healing took place in his mind first, and then transferred to his body."

As word about his "miraculous cures" had leaked out, his reputation as a "healing" man had spread rapidly, but Rev himself was far from complacent about his success. If anything, it made him clamp his jaws in even greater **determination** to find the source of this tremendous enigma one way or the other. He had to find out about this healing principle, which apparently constituted the essence of his success. In his quest for an answer, he travelled all over the country, visiting various Shrines, and attending healing services in many churches, religious sects, etc. "Healing came about as a result of shouting, rolling, talking in tongues, complete silence, or just the laying on or touching of hands," Rev said. "In many cases healing did in fact take place, and while I could see the obvious results of such healing, the *principle* eluded me."

Finally Rev heard about CONCEPT-THERAPY. He went down to its headquarters in Texas and it did not take him very long to find out that it had all of the answers that he had been looking for so long. So once more he changed his career, but this time was the last, for after all his searching, Rev had finally found his place.

Katherine Calhoun changed her career, too. In a talk entitled "Calhoun before and after CONCEPT-THER-APY," Kathy said that; "as a child, some religious teachings did not make sense to me. Coming from a very religious family, I was a devout little girl, and went to Church every Sunday. There were three girls in our family, and we loved to fight. When Mom wanted us to be good she'd say: "Now you won't go to heaven if you don't stop fighting, 'cause there's no fighting there." One day I shocked my mother out of her wits by telling her that if that was true that I didn't want to go to heaven, because I just loved to fight. Mother, gasping for breath, blurted out: "why, you shouldn't say things like that!" And so I stopped asking questions, but I *thought* just the same; those wheels kept turning. Through the progressing years, there was still a burning quest to know more about religious matters and after I grew up I was elected National secretary of the ......* youth group — we travelled all over the country trying to unite all young people into one basic religion. Imagine the presumptuousness! Trying to get all those people to look at things one way — the —* way!" she bristled. "Well, that didn't last long! Then I went to college, and majored in religious subjects. After that I went back to work again. I had a good job, a good salary, I was looked up to in the community, and yet, at night I would go home and feel an emptiness. I would say, "well, what's the use of this? Something is missing. There's got to be some answers to the questions I still have." Then back to college I went, studying more religion. I got a master's degree and a certification, but it didn't give me any more answers. I was still empty.

Than I heard about CONCEPT-THERAPY. A friend told me to get to San Antonio as soon as I could, because I still had all of my questions.

I came to the Ranch in 1950. The first thing I noticed people doing down here was walking around to music." (Kathy is referring here to the SLUMP, which is a form of musical therapy used by CONCEPT-THERAPY.) The letters stand for: "Souls Live Upon Many Planes." I asked Dr. Fleet; What are they doing? and he answered: "This is the way we train our students in the art of CONCEN-TRATION. The mind is like an unruly steed going in all directions, and a person cannot learn to get in tune with the POWER that is WITHIN unless he's trained in the art of CONCENTRATION." Well, said Kathy, "here I was with a master's degree and I'd never been trained in that! Being a proud person," she went on, "it took me a long time to get used to the system they use down here to

_____
* Name of this religion deliberately omitted to avoid possible offense.

get a person to know himself, and sometimes it was difficult to swallow, because it was in direct contradiction to what I'd been trained in. By and by, though, I began to realize that I had found what I had been looking for. Something within me had been vibrating — it was kind of like the man who was lost in the desert, and who would die any moment unless he would find some water. Suddenly he finds his life-giving water and he drinks of it. The only thing I could say after taking CONCEPT-THERAPY, is that it was like a person finding life-giving water. I learned about the laws and little by little I learned to apply them. After that, I never could go back into my church position. I'd like to tell you of a few things I found here that did revolutionize my life, when I began to understand that working with *ideas* is the thing that we should be concerned with. Wasn't it Victor Hugo who said: "Greater than all the armies in the world is an idea whose time has come?" Now I'd never known that the ideas we hold become so impregnated into the very fibers of our nature that our body, mind and soul, yes our very life and environment, become the field in which these ideas grow and express. Slowly I began to understand that the ideas I'd held in my own life had brought about unrest, unhappiness and sickness, and slowly but surely the BIG IDEA began to dawn upon me. I had *created* my condition, and I could change my life by *creating* another one. The Creative Principle is one of the greatest things the CONCEPT-THERAPY student gains."

Shifting gear, Kathy said: "Now I'd like to talk a little bit about the outer world and the inner world. All our lives we were taught about the outer world, such as hairdos, putting make-up on our faces, etc.," she said, turning to the ladies, "but we were taught nothing about the inner world. BCT, which means Before CONCEPT-THERA-PY, I was in a pit of ignorance about the inner world. Now CONCEPT-THERAPY takes you on a journey and helps you find treasures of the higher realm of Consciousness, referred to by some as Cosmic Consciousness, Nirvana, the Kingdom of Heaven, the Fourth Dimension, etc. Very logically CONCEPT-THERAPY begins to show you the Unknown Power Within, and they refer to it as the "X," (signifying that to the human mind it is unknowable—and it says in the Bible that the finite mind cannot comprehend the Infinite) which appealed to me. CONCEPT-THER-APY says let's go to the science books, and begin to follow the line of Consciousness. Let's say that if in the beginning there was a Power — that was all-powerful, and had all the knowledge, and was everywhere present—then that Power must have started working way back there with some sort of an IMAGE of a world that was to be created; It must have planned a "blue print," and then It must have had the ability to begin to manifest Its Idea. We might say that I had the ability to originate the Image, as well as the ability to PLAN out a SYSTEM by which It could manifest Its Image in the Universe. It then went through the electronic, mineral, vegetable and animal stages, and finally It came to man, as yet the highest of creation." Her eyes twinkling, she said: "Remember the statement in the Bible, which says: And God said, let US create Man in OUR Image, and after OUR Likeness?" Now *that* got me to thinking—because what did it *mean* when it said: Let *Us* make Man in *Our* Image? And again CONCEPT-THERAPY came along and explained to me that within this CREATIVE POWER there must have been BOTH an ORIGINATIVE and an EXECUTIVE element. (This corresponds with the male and female principle, as explained in the Hermetic teachings under the law of gender, which law is covered in detail in Concept-Therapy). Now if that were true, and man were made in the Image of this IMAGE-MAKER — the Great Architect of the Universe — then it must mean that Man also was a "little creator," a "little image-maker," and slowly but gradually, CONCEPT-THER-APY begins to break these parts of human personality down in a lesson that's called "The Factors of Personality," and it begins to show how due to faulty reasoning a person originates wrong concepts, selects wrong or negative things for his body — because he's not been given a reasonable explanation of the laws of his body— and then selects the wrong thoughts for his mind, and finally engages in the selection of wrong acts. Now the Great Power Within says: "ASK AND YOU SHALL RE-CEIVE," and CONCEPT-THERAPY teaches you how to ask properly so that you can utilize this Power on the positive side—for to the Power it matters not whether what you ask is on the positive or the negative side. It carries out what you ask, whether you are aware of it or not.

What if through ignorance you ask? It makes no difference, for this Great Power within is an Executive Power, just like electricity. You might be ignorant of the laws of electricity, and it doesn't matter whether you're the best person or the greatest saint on earth, if you don't know how to use it, it can knock you dead just as easily as it will run an appliance for you — because it is no respector of persons. I tell you, my friends, that was pretty hard medicine for me to take! To think that there's a Power that is within us, which operates under exact law like electricity, and It is no respector of persons! (human personalities, that is.) In respect to this Power, many of us are like the savage who did not understand electricity, and who therefore thought he saw a miracle when he turned a switch and the room lit up for him.

So CONCEPT-THERAPY began to show me in a very logical manner that there is a Power within us, that operates in much the same way that electricity does, and that there are Laws governing it; and to the degree that a man can understand those Laws and can apply them in his life — then the Power Within will serve the man! (To give a few examples of men who have understood the workings of this Power but have applied it in the "bad" or negative sense we quote such names as Napoleon, Mussolini, Hitler, etc. In so doing, however, they overlooked another great Law, and that is that by consistent application of the Power in a negative, destructive sense, we ultimately destroy ourselves, and their tragic endings attest to this fact. The implications are just as valid in the opposite sense, however, in that by consistent application of the Law in the constructive, positive sense, we ultimately raise ourselves to a God-like level. Here we can quote such names as Schweitzer, Whitman, Gautama, Jesus, etc.) Over and over this Big Idea was laid down: There is a Power that rules the universe, It is within you, and It can be contacted and directed. You don't have to wait until you die, because this Power is here now, within you. Then CONCEPT-THERAPY began to show us how to begin to utilize this power within on the positive side of life. Dr. Higdon didn't just tell us to "just think positively," but laid down a very simple, mathematical formula regarding this Power. I felt as though the whole Universe had been opened up to me when I left here; new realms of thought and action that I had never dreamed existed, and there was HOPE that I could attain to a higher state of consciousness. The beauty of it was that it could be attained through KNOWLEDGE, *proper* knowledge, that is. So I began to gather knowledge of the INNER WORLD, and as a man begins to originate —"As a man thinketh in his heart"—(subconsciously) so he becomes. "Ask and ye shall receive," it says in the Bible. Here eyes twinkling, she turned to the audience and queried: "Suppose you asked for a room light to come on?" "When the proper *hookup* has been made—such as switches, wires connections and lamp, it is no mystery. You simply flip the switch, and — the proper *hookup* or *connection* having been established previously — the light comes on for you. So it does take a little time to get our *hookup* to the Power established; first we must rid ourselves of some faulty hookups that we've established," (such as wrong, limiting concepts, erroneous ideas, "hang-ups" etc.), "I came to fully realize that everything in the universe is governed by law." (Any true scientist, astronomer, and mathematical genius will readily attest to this fact. Einstein, for instance, once said: "While I cannot believe in God, I *do* believe in a great Something, a Power, which is very logical, orderly and lawful"). "Hm," she said, "I hadn't been taught that in my religious training! But when I began to understand *this* it began to make the training religion tried to give me understandable!

The last lesson in CONCEPT-THERAPY points out to

the students that *nothing escapes the law* — there isn't a "place, condition, individual or group that's exempt from law. The crystal dewdrop, the gentle zephyr, the shimmering wavelet, the fleecy cloud and the resplendent sunset are all just as they are in accordance with the mandates of law." Then we began to understand that the scientist had worked with law all along. Dr. Fleet said that the law is so exacting that they can tell you the very day to look for Haley's comet to return — which takes some eighty years to travel a cycle! Think about that! Scientists have charted the courses of the planets. Today we begin to realize that if law is so exacting in *every phase of creation,* doesn't it stand to reason that man, too, should be governed by law? Yes, we maintain that man thinks, he wills, he imagines, and he develops physically, mentally, and spiritually, all in accordance with the mandates of LAW. At times, someone asks: "If the law is inescapable, then are we just the helpless victims of a universal system, every detail of which is unavoidable and inevitable?" "Oh, no," we say, "Man, you are not the VICTIM of a system, but you are a potential VICTOR, and man should come to the place where he understands that he is a little creator made in the image of the Big Creator, and that it's his prerogative and right to begin to take his rightful inheritance—his share of utilization of that Power—in accordance with Its Laws."

"There's much research being done in the realms of outer space, but very little inwardly. The mission of the CONCEPT-THERAPY movement is to show man how to turn his consciousness inwardly, and to research and develop his inner space, resources and potential. You know, I started in this movement in 1950, when they had a big convention, and I was so enraptured with this great new thing I'd found that I went back and within a short while I was here again to be on the staff. Before long I was sent out as a secretary on the Dr. and Mrs. Whittenberg, and Reverend Crump teaching teams. I went out as a secretary — not as a teacher. But I "got tricked into" teaching, because Reverend Crump was left to teach alone one time and he asked me, "Would you help me teach?," and I had a very 'good' concept, she said facetiously. I said, "Oh, no sir, I could *not* do that!" She then added one of her favorite jokes: "Blessed are those who think they cannot do something, for they shall not be disappointed!" (This is an appropriate adaptation from Dr. Fleet's contention that "Blessed are those who expect nothing, for they shall not be disappointed!"). "And you know what?," she continued, "I couldn't teach!" I said, "Rev., I will read that lesson but I don't know what it means!" So after a while he said: "*Miss Calhoun, take stock of yourself! What are you telling yourself?*" Hm — soon I began to look at some of my concepts and little by little I began to figure out what the lessons of CONCEPT-THERAPY meant. And, so, ever since then, I've been digging, and in the space of sixteen years I had the pleasure of helping to teach in over four hundred classes in the United States and Canada; and you know, each time we teach a class it's like the first time we taught it — it's that fresh and new every time. There's just that much depth to CONCEPT-THERAPY. It's a great venture — in our classes we have protestants, jews, catholics, agnostics, atheists, you name it — all kinds of people, and all of them without exception find something in CONCEPT-THERAPY, that strengthens their faith in life. I re-

member one class in which a man came up to me and said:
"I don't know whether I'd be welcome in your class or
not!" I asked him why. He said, "because I am an atheist."
I said: "Shake hands, brother, you will probably be our
best student!" "Oh?" he gasped. I said, "yes, because you
have already dared to openly challenge the fallacies and
limitations of the God-concept that's been handed to you,
so you don't mind going around telling people that you
can't believe in the God about whom you were taught, and
as such you ought to be among the first to grasp the BIG
IDEA in the class we're teaching." In amazement, he said:
"Well, that's exactly right!" He grasped the BIG IDEA
all right. Not only did he grasp it, but he was so enthu-
siastic that in a week he went back home, organized a
class and we gained 25 new students from this so-called
atheist, she added affectionately. "Well," he said, "this
idea that you're teaching about this Power is what I've
thought all my life, and people said that I was an infidel."
He just was looking for a broader concept — a logical
concept — of this Power.

And so we would say that all people who come into our
classes — hindus, mohammedans, you name it, all gain
something very worthwhile. In fact a mohammedan wrote
me and said, "why this work correlates perfectly with my
training." We recently had a man from Singapore who
delayed his trip back home in order to stay in Toronto to
take CONCEPT-THERAPY. This man, a buddhist, said:
"Why, you've taught me in one course the answer that has
eluded me in my religion!" So we would say that when a
person begins to understand the laws which we teach,
and begins to inculcate them into his life, that invariably
the person's health improves, as does his ability to get

along in business, with associates, with friends, etc. And I might just say this—that sort of as a "bonus" in CONCEPT-THERAPY, I "got Health." She spelled it: H-E-A-L-T-H. "I came sick in spiritual knowledge, and in its wake came Health. If you'd all have a few hours, I'd tell you what I was like B.C.T. (Before CONCEPT-THERAPY). I can't tell you how many ailments I had. One of them was that I was allergic to 50 different foods and items and objects and took up to 21 different allergy shots every day. I even brought my little bottles and my hypodermic syringe with me, and when I came here Dr. Fleet said: "Sure we have some people who can give you your shots." But they didn't give me that kind of shots — oh, no, they gave me a different kind — right up in my brain cells. I kept wondering what the silly system was they had down here of teaching people to find a new Way of Life. So I got stuck with it. You know," she said confidentially, "one of the things I was allergic to was chocolate — so B.C.T. I did without it for 10 years — but now (A.C.T., (After CONCEPT-THERAPY) I always say to the waitress, "any flavor ice-cream, please, just so it's chocolate!" Now before CONCEPT-THERAPY I took all of these shots, had $1000.00 in doctor bills, but I didn't get better. I withheld eating foods I "shouldn't" eat, I stopped taking shots and I got better. Now, somebody might say that that must have been one of those disturbances that was not of a physical origin — one of those that fall into the 80 or 90%, and that's why Dr. Fleet said: "Taking physical treatment will not help you, you must be taught about the Inner Life, the Healer Within, etc. The concept they've been giving you as to what you're allergic to, the battle that's been going on between your inherited self and your acquired self, etc." So — I think that's a pretty wonderful bonus, don't you? Health! Her eyes sparkled. "I didn't know I was going to find Health when I came here! I came seeking spiritual knowledge—and I think now I'm just about the healthiest person in the world. I've got that CONCEPT now! They helped me change my THINKING down here, and changed my CONCEPTS, and now I've got the CONCEPT that I'm one of the healthiest people in the world. Now, in closing, I'd like to say this:

There's a story in the Bible that tells about a man who found a treasure in a field, and he forthwith went out and sold all that he had in order that he might come and buy the field; I guess so he could dig and dig a little more, and that's what I like to think of in CONCEPT-THERAPY — that when we come into a class of instruction, it's just like we see a big treasure in a field, and we just can't scoop all of them up at once and put them in a box because there's too many treasures, so we want to go back and dig more, for then we can travel on the Path of Knowledge and get more of the treasures that are higher up on the Path.

So like the man in the book says: "Once you have found the way, it will obsess you, but it will be a magnificent obsession!"

How right she is. Nothing in the world can be worth as much as the health-giving qualities, the peace, the contentment, the satisfaction, and the *feeling* of being at home in the Universe which CONCEPT-THERAPY gives to its students.

I could continue to pile testimony upon testimony, and tell you the stories of Fred and Opal Striffler, Nettie Bergen, Ray and Margie Scroggins, Dr. and Mrs. Sessions, and so on ad infinitum, but I cannot give you the *experience* for yourself, for there are no shortcuts when it comes to *experience*. All I can do is tell you about that which became a new Way of Life for me and thousands of others, and which will become a new Way of Life for you, too, should you decide to enroll. I could only tell you of some techniques within these pages, but I can't provide for you the warmth and interest of the people in this movement or the tremendous stimulation you'll receive in the proper learning environment provided by the classes. I can't hope to duplicate within these pages the results of the forty years of detailed research by Dr. Fleet, possibly the most human person I have ever met. I can only give you the Ideas, not the:

VISION

A tribe of Indians had no contact with the outside world. The old chief, before he died, wished to choose the young man who would be chief after him. He called together the young braves of the tribe and said, "See yonder peak? You will climb that mountain and each one bring back something to show how far he has climbed.

By and by one young brave came back, "O Chief," he said, "I have travelled to where the fields end, and I have brought back a grain of wheat." The chief said to him, "Go shoot the arrow and wrestle with the wild ox, and strengthen thyself." Another young brave returned. "O

Chief, I have travelled beyond the fields of grain, and I have brought back this last branch of the last tree." The Chief replied to this one as he had the first. Then another returned. "O Chief, I have travelled past the cultivated fields, through the trees, and came to a place where there was no living thing, and it was cold, and I was afraid. I have brought this stone." He received the same reply as the first.

So during the long day the young men kept coming back, some with one thing and some another, until it grew dark. The last man burst into the circle by the fire. His face was shining as he said, "O Chief, I travelled beyond the fields and the trees until I came to the snow, and I struggled through the snow to the mountain peak. I have brought back nothing, but I have seen the Sea."

The old Chief said, "My people, this is the young man who will be chief when I am gone. He is worthy to lead you. He has seen a VISION."

New Chronicle

Indeed, dear reader, I can't tell you how to reason with your soul and feelings, besides your intellect, or tell you how to determine where you want to go — plan it out — and go there. Only you—given the proper knowledge, can do that. I can't tell you how to lose your problems and the skepticism that gives rise to them, for all of this can only be accomplished through personal experience, and I can't provide you with the *experience,* for that must be uniquely your own.

I join Ernest Holmes in saying that Peace stands at the door of your consciousness and awaits your acceptance of It. However, it does not stand outside your door, waiting for entrance, so much as it stands inside waiting to be expressed in everything you do.

CONCEPT-THERAPY will give you the Knowledge, which is the key to Peace, and it's available to you all over the United States and Canada. Since it's fully guaranteed, and you have nothing to lose but your objections, why not listen to the Voice of Your True Self; yes, why not try CONCEPT-THERAPY. Peace Be With You.

CONCEPT-THERAPY INSTITUTE
Route 8, Box 250
San Antonio, Texas